If this family and their cute dog were looking for a place to see dozens of neon signs all at once, they could hardly have done better than this staged photo on Chattanooga's Broad Street. Besides the Holiday Inn–inspired behemoth belonging to the Albert Pick Motel, in the distance, see if you can spot a typical drive-in of the day (the Maypole) and a Kayo gas station, among other signage stretching into the distance. *Rock City collection.*

The chain of Kay's Ice Cream (aka Kay's Kastles) parlors had dozens of locations throughout Tennessee and adjoining states, but its most identifiable feature was the behemoth ice-cream cone above the roofs. Several of the cones survived even as the Kay's chain melted, but rarely seen nowadays is the proportionately giant boy with the protruding tongue. *John Margolies collection.*

VINTAGE

TENNESSEE SIGNS

TIM HOLLIS

Published by The History Press
Charleston, SC
www.historypress.com

Cover images courtesy of the author except back cover, top right: Debra Jane Seltzer collection.

Unless otherwise noted, all images are courtesy of the author.

First published 2022

Manufactured in the United States

ISBN 9781467151801

Library of Congress Control Number: 2022933411

CONTENTS

Zeige's
BAKERY
LOAN
OFFICE
LOANS
LUGGAGE
JEWELERS

ACKNOWLEDGEMENTS

Although most of the material you will see in the pages that follow originated in my own decades-long collection of memorabilia, credit must be given to the additional sources that enlivened the result. As you will notice in the credit lines for the photos, a number of them (as well as other helpful information) came from fellow tourism collectors, historians and photographers: Zap Actiondowner, John Baeder, Rebecca Burrum, Al Coleman, Loren "Yogi" Jones, Vance Lauderdale, Ruth Matthews, the staff (past and present) at Rock City Gardens, Debra Jane Seltzer (www.roadarch.com), Mitzi Soward and Russell Wells.

We must also acknowledge the late photographer John Margolies, who bequeathed his personal archive to the Library of Congress with the amazing stipulation that no restrictions be imposed on its use by other authors and researchers.

OPPOSITE: Market Street, downtown Chattanooga's main shopping district, was geared more toward locals than tourists, and its years of development resulted in signs of many different decades being jammed together. Note that they range from possible 1930s or 1940s neon signage to modern 1960s plastic signs with the actual lighting inside.

Conner
MOTOR
LODGE
PORCHES OVER RIVER

Cumberland
AIR CONDITIONED
MOTEL
NO VACANCY
TV

INTRODUCTION

This book had one of the strangest beginnings of the thirty-five previous ones I have done. Way back in 2008, I was responsible for an Arcadia Publishing volume titled *Vintage Birmingham Signs*. As the simple title indicated, this was a collection of images of the various types of signage that made up the commercial landscape of my beloved Birmingham, Alabama. The emphasis was on neon signs, as I was able to tap into the archives of several defunct sign companies that had nevertheless maintained quite remarkable photographic archives of their long-ago work.

Then, in 2009, another piece of the puzzle fell into place quite by accident. My History Press publication *See Rock City: The Story of Rock City Gardens* was a revised and polished version of an unpublished manuscript from 1991. During the writing of the original text, I had been largely responsible for organizing Rock City's vast but somewhat confusing archival materials. When the work resumed in 2008–9, I had to revisit that collection, but things had changed in the publishing business, in that we now used digital scans of images. By necessity, Rock City had to allow me to cart their voluminous scrapbooks and boxes of photos home to Alabama to scan the needed ones for the new book.

OPPOSITE: Motel signage had the task of luring travelers who were either already in a tourist center—such as the Conner Motor Lodge in the Smoky Mountains—or on their way to one, as with the Cumberland Motel in Clarksville. **Bottom** *Al Coleman collection.*

This is a terrific and typical example of the kind of photo that lurked in Rock City's archives. The photographer was documenting the "1/3 Mile to Highway 58" sign and its accompanying birdhouse at far right but captured quite a

conglomeration of other signage as US 41 crept its way around the base of Lookout Mountain. *Rock City collection.*

Now, in the 1950s, 1960s and 1970s, when Rock City's roadside marketing was at its peak, the attraction employed professional photographers to go out and document its signage across the Tennessee countryside. By that time, the famous barn roofs were already beginning to disappear, so most of the photography involved billboards. Because the photographers sought to capture not only the Rock City signs but also the look of the area in which they were placed, most of the photos showed numerous other forms of signage—for motels, restaurants, other attractions, gas stations and so on. The photographs' biggest drawback was that most of them had neither a date nor a location recorded; any information of that type, if it existed at all, had to be gleaned from studying internal evidence in the photos. Nonetheless, with the success of *Vintage Birmingham Signs* fresh on my mind, while scanning the Rock City book material, I also filed away any images I thought I might be able to use in a possible *Vintage Chattanooga Signs* book.

Once I had all of my deadlines met, I decided to check into the possibility of doing the Chattanooga book. Unfortunately, one of the things I found is that there were apparently no Chattanooga equivalents to the Birmingham neon sign companies that had saved so many photos. I gathered as many postcards and other items as I could to add to what I had gotten from Rock City, but when I exhausted all avenues, I still did not have enough to make the bare minimum of images required for such a book. Therefore, I simply saved them on disk and put it away in a desk drawer.

Finally, in 2021, after spending several years on the volumes in the *Lost Attractions* series (don't worry, folks, there are more of those to come), I began to wonder if I could expand the Chattanooga signs idea to cover the entire state and thus have enough material. That was indeed what happened, and the result is now before your wondering eyes. Because the book began with Chattanooga, you will still notice a heavy amount of material from that area, and since I have done several books on tourism history in the Great Smoky Mountains, I also had images left over that I could finally put to use here. The rest of Tennessee was assembled one piece at a time, like a giant statewide jigsaw puzzle.

So, now that you know how it all began, please continue to the next page to see how it all wound up.

ONE

WHAT'S IN STORE FOR US?

Any of the topics covered in this book could just as easily have been the subject of the first chapter, but we have chosen to begin with an experience familiar to practically everyone. The very idea of shopping can fall into many forms, ranging from large downtown department stores to small-town Main Streets with their five-and-ten-cent stores (renamed variety stores after their merchandise no longer cost five or ten cents).

But those forms of stores are not the end of the list of categories. What about grocery stores? There were small neighborhood grocers aplenty, and they eventually faced competition from giant supermarkets, which offered aisles and aisles of every conceivable edible. And there were drugstores. Those, too, were neighborhood affairs, even when affiliated with a national chain such as Rexall. Clothing stores of various types served those who perhaps did not have the finances or the constitution to face the upscale department stores. And in tourist areas—of which Tennessee had plenty, as we all know—souvenir and gift shops bloomed to help separate those "touristers" from any money that had not already been taken by meals, gas, lodging and entertainment. (Don't worry, we'll get to those four categories as we move along.)

In case you haven't already figured it out, the one thing all of these businesses had in common was a need to let the public know they were there. That is where their signage became most important, as it would have been quite impossible to get customers through the doors unless the customers could find them in the first place. We are about to see a number of different ways that businesses went about doing that, and you just might encounter some of your own favorite shopping haunts along the way.

TOP: There is no better place to begin our shopping trip than in a classic downtown area, as pictured here in Memphis around 1936. In the distance, note the huge vertical sign for Goldsmith's department store and, of course, the magnificent marquee of the Loew's State Theater. Interestingly, while the buildings on the left-hand side of this photo survive today, none of the ones on the right exist anymore.

OPPOSITE, BOTTOM: We're still in Memphis, but more than a decade later and a few blocks north of the previous view. A Walgreens drugstore is notable, as it has basically the same logo the chain uses today. As with all the other defunct retailers, historians bemoan the loss of the Warner Theater in the center of this shot; it was demolished in the 1960s for a bank tower.

ABOVE: Since we've visited Memphis, let's zoom to the other side of the state and drop in on Market Street in Chattanooga. The plentiful neon signs are emblematic of downtown shopping, but note the signage for the S.H. Kress variety store in the middle of the block. We will be seeing a lot more of Kress in the pages that follow. You can also see that those major tourist highways—US 27, US 11 and US 64—converged at this intersection.

DRAPER & DARWIN

WHITE'S AUTO

OPPOSITE, TOP: Here is another Chattanooga angle with so much signage that it's hard to take it all in. By squinting and peering, see if you can find the signs for the Rogers and Dixie Theaters, Hotel Patten, a classic Gulf service station and rooftop billboards for Royal Crown Cola, Fleetwood Coffee, Sterling Beer and U.S. Royal Tires, among others.

OPPOSITE, MIDDLE: Small towns had their packed retail districts as well. The photographer in Union City, in the extreme northwestern corner of Tennessee, risked being flattened by traffic to capture this view of the town's stores, including the red letters of a Ben Franklin 5 & 10 store on the right.

OPPOSITE, BOTTOM: Jonesboro is acknowledged as the oldest city in Tennessee, and its small retail center resembles something out of a Hallmark movie. The Coca-Cola sign on the White's building is a classic, with its blue and green diamonds. Farther down, on the opposite side of the street, is another small-town fixture, Western Auto.

ABOVE: Bristol is known for its main drag, State Street, straddling the Tennessee/Virginia state line, as indicated by the overhead sign in the distance. If you can tear your gaze away from the Cameo Theater marquee, about halfway up the block, on the right, you may spy yet another Kress store.

KRESS

PARK
BANK
Miller's

OPPOSITE, TOP: Here is that same Kress building as it looks today. The Kress chain began in Tennessee (Memphis, 1896), and the varying architectural styles of its former buildings have made them valuable assets for preservationists. More often than not, even as the buildings have been converted into other uses, at least some of the distinctive Kress signage has been kept in place.

OPPOSITE, BOTTOM: Naturally, nothing could beat a downtown shopping area during the Christmas season. Some photographer was lucky to get this view of Knoxville in 1952 with all the street decorations in place, plus the Miller's department store with its halls suitably decked with boughs of holly. It looks like a surprisingly light day for traffic, however.

ABOVE: As retail moved from downtowns into suburban shopping centers, old-time retailers were forced to go along. Loveman's was a longtime fixture in Chattanooga (not directly related to the Loveman's store chain in Birmingham). This was the architect's rendering of its new location at Eastgate Mall.

HARVEYS . . . Nashville's Largest and Oldest Department Store

while in Nashville, do as Nashvillians do

enjoy Harveys!

Tennessee's Leading Stores

HARVEYS HAS IT . . . and Harveys will charge it, wrap it, mail it, or—if need be—exchange it. All with good cheer.

OPPOSITE: In Nashville, Harvey's was a major name in the department store game. In addition to its regular signage, Harvey's was known for its collection of antique carousel horses rescued from the city's defunct Glendale Park. They were placed throughout the store and, as seen here, became a part of the logo found in newspaper and magazine ads. As with so many downtown fixtures across the country, the flagship Harvey's closed (in 1984).

ABOVE: Swinging back to Memphis, we boogie down to Beale Street. Unfortunately, by the time this twilight shot was taken, things had gotten a bit seedy. There appear to be more darkened buildings and doorways than might be considered strictly safe. However, Beale eventually came booming back and now takes its deserved place in music and cultural history.

TOP: After the Grand Ole Opry's debut in 1925, the live radio broadcast moved into, and then outgrew, several Nashville facilities. In 1943, it took up residence in a former tabernacle known as the Ryman Auditorium. Here we can see just a portion of the crowd waiting for the show, as well as a terrific view of the Opry's charmingly homemade-style signage.

OPPOSITE, BOTTOM: This postcard view dates from 1958, when the Opry waiting line had grown to a prodigious size. The postcard company blurred most of the signage except a couple of loan shops and a paint store. Within a few years, this area, around Fifth Avenue and Broadway, deteriorated into sleaze, with porn shops and other unsavory businesses lining the streets. The Opry moved to its new home at Opryland USA in 1974. Today, most of these same buildings still exist, but they have been converted into entertainment venues with a remarkable number of retro-style neon signs they did not have in their previous lives.

ABOVE: Several blocks away from the Ryman Auditorium, Printer's Alley developed its own set of nightspots, which brightened the streetscape considerably with their multitude of signs. This brochure shows how it looked at just about the time the Opry was departing downtown for its new life in the suburbs.

The signs and billboards on Chattanooga's Broad Street in the mid-1960s were something else. Rock City's photographer tasked with documenting the Mother Goose Village billboard could not have known that it would be just as historic as JFG Coffee, Cloogman's Big Scramble and ABC Liquors. *Rock City collection.*

OPPOSITE, TOP: By the 1980s, Broad Street had become home to antique stores, one of which occupied the former Cloogman's/ABC Liquors building. Outside rested this relic of a bygone day, its original home unknown. As we saw a few pages ago, Western Auto was once the Dollar General of its day, with stores in towns large, small and minuscule.

OPPOSITE, BOTTOM: There was a time when neon signs could be found identifying all sorts of retail businesses. This one in Bristol, photographed in 2011, would have been a beauty with its neon flowers. It has since withered on the vine and gone to seed. *Debra Jane Seltzer collection.*

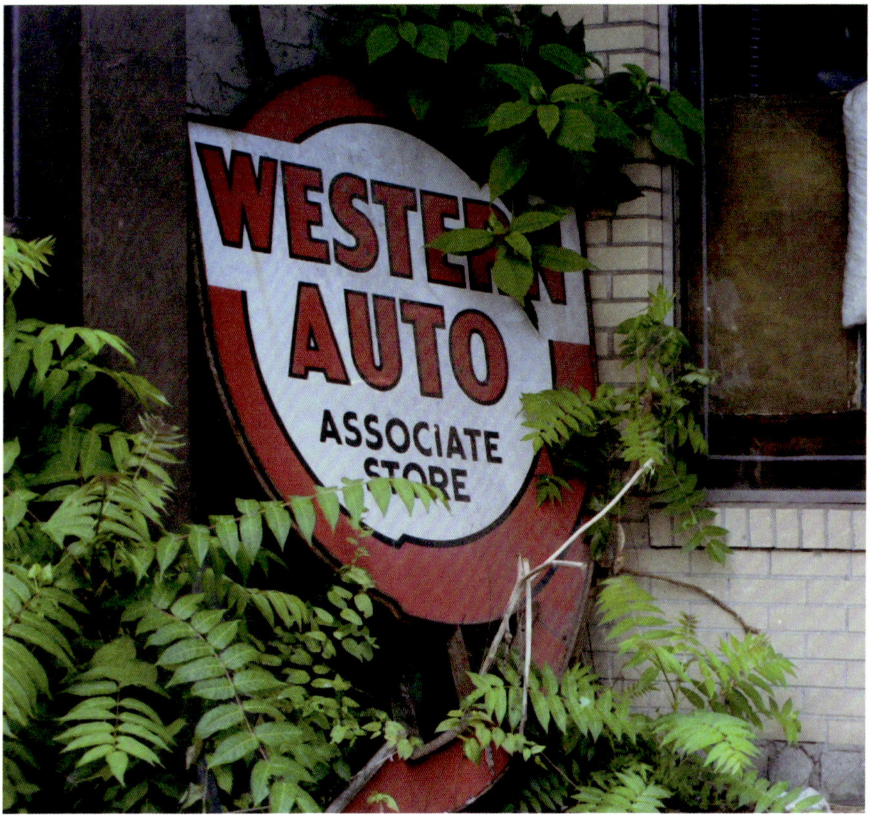
WESTERN
AUTO
ASSOCIATE
STORE

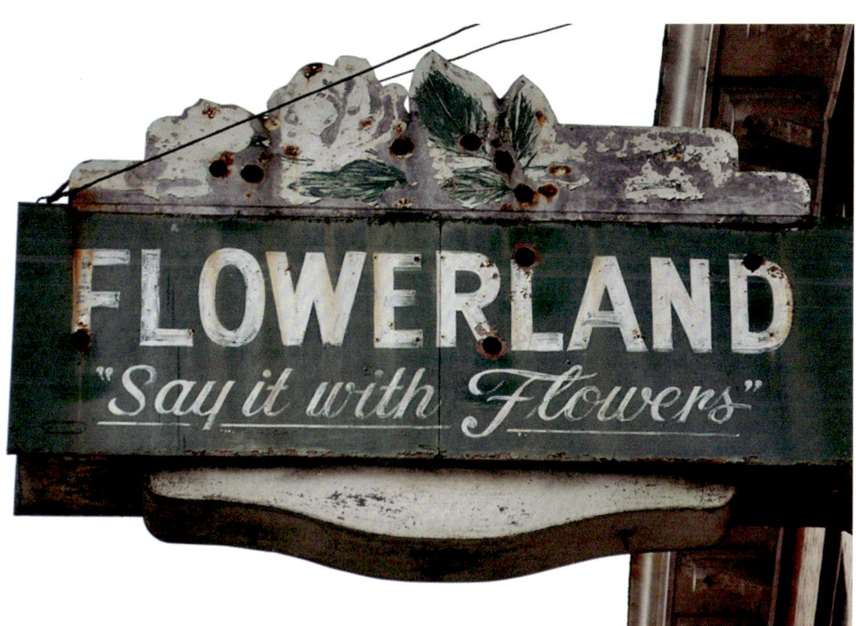

FLOWERLAND
"Say it with Flowers"

The owner of the Soap Opera Laundry must have had a bubbly sense of humor when it came time to name the business. The exact age of this sign is unknown, but photographer Debra Jane Seltzer found it in Nashville in 2007. She reports that, seven years later, its lettering and neon had all been removed. *Debra Jane Seltzer collection.*

OPPOSITE: No, that isn't the annoying gag gift Big Mouth Billy Bass on this Nashville neon spectacular. It dates to the early 1950s, long before Billy was a gleam in some demented inventor's eye. Unfortunately, no one has been able to fish for this fish since the sign was removed in 2009. *Debra Jane Seltzer collection.*

NASHVILLE
SPORTING
GOODS

BIG
STAR
Maxwell's

OPPOSITE: The signs for the chain of Big Star grocery stores illustrated a custom almost unheard of today. Besides the standard logo, each sign also included the franchise owner's name as part of the neon. That indicated a sense of permanence that most businesses with a high turnover of ownership could not even imagine. This Maxwell's Big Star in Bolivar was still in business as of this writing. *Debra Jane Seltzer collection.*

ABOVE: Groceries such as Big Star were the forerunners of the giant supermarkets that emerged in post–World War II America. Knoxville-based Cas Walker had quite a reputation in East Tennessee, in more ways than one. But he gained his place in history when his local TV show served as the public's introduction to budding young singer Dolly Parton.

Signs advertising grocery products could come in many different forms. This lighted clock featured the Elm Hill Meats cartoon lumberjack, who sang, "I'm Elm Hill Bill, I'm big and strong / I chop down elm trees all day long / And each of these I place with a smack / On an Elm Hill Quality All-Meat Pack."

OPPOSITE: Another catchy jingle appeared in the commercials for Jackson's Kelly Foods, mainly known for its canned chili. Animated cartoon leprechauns danced a jig: "Things are cookin' at the Kellys / Home-cooked meals are at the Kellys / Heat an' serve 'em in a minute, they're so good, good good." Gettin' hungry yet, now are ye? *Debra Jane Seltzer collection.*

K
KELLY FOODS

Cream City
ICE CREAM

DRUGS
BY-RYT
SUPER MARKET
POTATOES
50 LBS 99¢
STOP
DRUGS

OPPOSITE, TOP: The Cream City Ice Cream rooftop sign in Cookeville has earned legendary status since it was first installed in 1950. In fact, that entire part of US 70 has been designated the Cream City Historic District, largely due to the preservation and appeal of that sign. Amazingly, the Cream City brand was out of business from 1986 to 2011, making it even more remarkable that the sign survived that period.

OPPOSITE, BOTTOM: This view of picturesquely named Hickory Valley shows the sign for another supermarket chain, By-Ryt, in close conjunction with a pharmacy sign that had cousins across the land. Apparently, neon sign companies loved creating overturned beakers that dripped medicine into mortars below, usually with an animated pestle to stir the concoction. *Rock City collection.*

ABOVE: Only those above a certain age will remember when Rexall was the largest drugstore chain of all. Each location had one of these trademark orange-and-blue signs, frequently including the owner's name (in the fashion we saw at the Big Star Grocery earlier). This one, photographed in Jellico in 2007, chose to simply use a location's name rather than an owner's.

There was no ignoring this remarkable neon creation at the foot of Lookout Mountain, near the bottom station of the Incline Railway. Unfortunately, the fancy lettering and dimensional mortar and animated pestle—no medication dripping this time—are long gone.

OPPOSITE: When these photos were taken, approximately ten years apart, Gatlinburg's downtown shopping district had not yet become a congested conglomeration of stores and traffic, but it was getting there fast. Look closely and you will be able to pick out numerous souvenir shops and other businesses that can no longer be seen, although their descendants continue to make the strip of US 441 a destination for tourists. *Both, Loren "Yogi" Jones collection.*

PARK
TOURIST
COURT
OFFICE
RESTAURANT
CHICKEN-STEAKS
SEAFOOD

NO
PARKING
ANY
TIME
MOTEL
DON WARD'S
GENUINE MOUNTAIN
HANDCRAFTS
CUSTOM
FURNITURE

How about these shopping choices at the base of Lookout Mountain? (In the background, note a car just beginning to make the climb to the top.) The Golden Gallon Milk Jug seems like a good place to pick up some refreshments to enjoy while you're spending the night at Johnson's Scenic Courts or staying home watching *The Flintstones* on your set from Incline Radio & TV. Yes, driving straight ahead instead of up the mountain would bring you to Flintstone, Georgia. *Rock City collection.*

TWO

CURLY CONES TO CRACKER BARRELS

All that shopping can certainly make one work up an appetite. Fortunately for fans of vintage signage, restaurants are our next stop along the way. As with the stores, eateries had a similar need to advertise their presence. More so than department stores or variety stores, restaurants depended on luring passersby who might not have originally set out to patronize them. If a colorful, flashing sign could work its magic on a growling stomach, that organ's owner was hooked.

We are about to see a remarkable cross-section of the roadside restaurant industry. Drive-ins seem to have made a special effort to stand out from their surroundings. Somehow, eating in one's car under the glow of a colorful neon sign seemed to make the curly topped soft ice cream taste even sweeter.

More upscale, full-service restaurants also made their signage into a major part of their roadside presence. Some of them survived for decades to become local landmarks; others might not be remembered today at all if not for the photos and postcards that preserve their images. The tourist areas, especially in the Great Smoky Mountains resorts, had a special challenge in that they had a captive audience—the job was convincing the visitors to give their cuisine a try.

Then there were chain restaurants nationally famous for hamburgers or fried chicken or any number of other specialties. Many of those will be seen in this chapter. And let us not ignore the fact that Tennessee gave the rest of the United States the ubiquitous Cracker Barrel chain, perhaps as emblematic and successful an edible enterprise as ever came from that state.

There was certainly nothing novel about calling a restaurant the Tennessean; there have been several of them over the years. The exact location of this one is unknown, although it was apparently on US 41 somewhere in the Monteagle area.

Across the street from the sign, note the billboard for Horne's, the chain of candy shops/restaurants that was the biggest competitor to Stuckey's in the 1960s. *Rock City collection.*

Some things can be just as memorable as a sign. This giant chef chicken has stood at the Shady Lawn Travel Center on I-65 at Ardmore for decades. The prodigious poultry has undergone numerous paint jobs, but this is how it looked in 1991. Today, it holds a different set of cutlery under its wings.

OPPOSITE: What could be more emblematic of the Tennessee hill country than this landmark at Church Hill? Even the combined efforts of the rifle-totin' mountaineer and Hillbilly Fried Chicken on the menu was not enough to keep the restaurant from closing in 2008. However, reports are that this masterpiece was not destroyed but currently belongs to a passionate collector. *Debra Jane Seltzer collection.*

TENNESSEE
the Mountaineer
RESTAURANT
FOR GOD SO
LOVED THE WORLD....
JOHN 3:16
Hillbilly
fried chicken

With the habit of postcard companies "enhancing" the photos from which their cards were printed, it's hard to say whether the Dixie Restaurant at Johnson City truly had that illuminated, billboard-sized graphic over its front entrance. If it did, we can imagine that it drew in traffic from far and wide traveling through the northeastern corner of the state.

OPPOSITE: This restaurant in the East Ridge section of Chattanooga began in 1953. As you can see, it survived to celebrate its fifty-first anniversary at the time this photo was taken. Unfortunately, it closed around the time of its fifty-seventh, although the sign remained in place for several years afterward. *Debra Jane Seltzer collection.*

Eidson
RESTAURANT
51 ST
ANNIVERSARY
HIGH
ENERGY
VEGETABLES
ECKERD
VISA
AMERICAN EXPRESS

It looks like an eighth dwarf, Hungry, failed to make the cut in Snow White's story, so he moved to Knoxville and opened his own restaurant. And no, that is not a typo on the sign: there really was (and still is, for that matter) a dairy known as French Broad, which conjures up all sorts of mental images.

OPPOSITE, TOP: On two of the major highways that brought tourists through Chattanooga, US 11 and US 64, the Gulas Restaurant was an art deco delight. Its two neon signs were augmented by the colorful billboard facing drivers in the parking lot.

OPPOSITE, BOTTOM: One of the many restaurants in Gatlinburg was the Open Hearth, which has survived in name but not in this location with its towering neon sign topped by a steer statue. And while human beings are somewhat outside the scope of this book, we cannot neglect to mention the waitstaff lined up like soldiers, ready to serve charcoal steaks at a moment's notice.

Gulas
RESTAURANT
RESTAURANT
STEAKS
BAR BQ
SEA FOODS

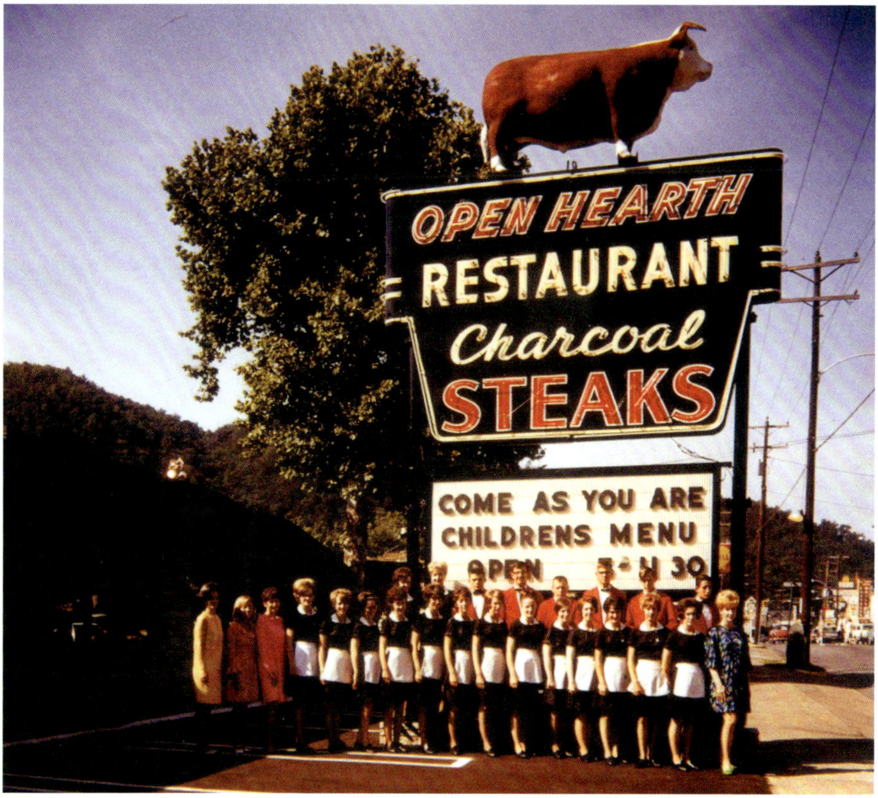

OPEN HEARTH
RESTAURANT
Charcoal
STEAKS
COME AS YOU ARE
CHILDRENS MENU

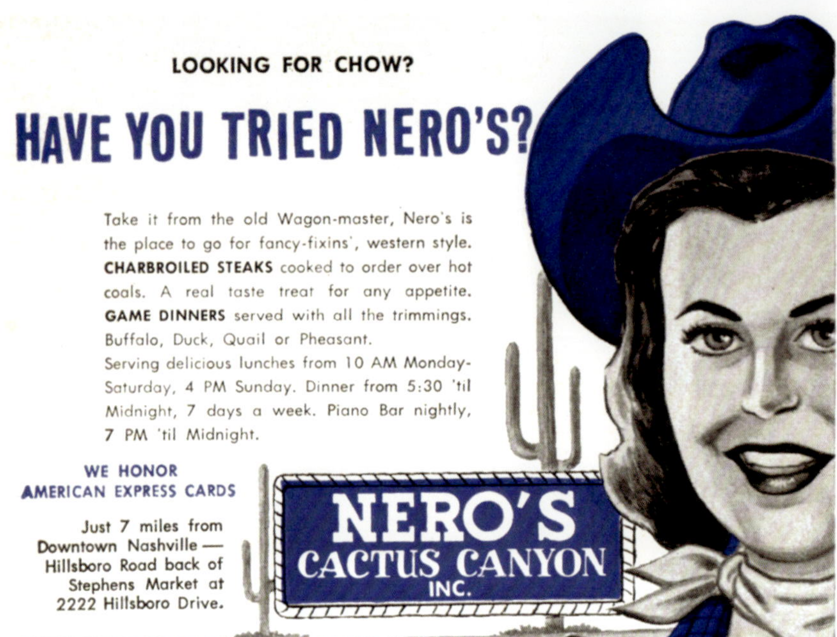

Somehow, the name of Roman emperor Nero does not seem to fit with a steakhouse called the Cactus Canyon, but it pulled up its chuck wagon in Nashville from 1958 to 1976 and became a local legend. This 1967 ad came about halfway through that sojourn. The smiling lady looks like she just came from the Opry stage yodeling, "I Wanna Be a Cowboy's Sweetheart."

OPPOSITE: Chain restaurants came to dominate the market, and one of the earliest was Howard Johnson's. It was not exaggerating when it adopted the slogan "From Maine to Florida." If you're good at mental jigsaw puzzles, your mind's eye may be able to reassemble the pieces of this Knoxville Howard Johnson's billboard that were repurposed to patch the end of a barn on US 441 near Seymour—a barn with one of the rapidly vanishing Rock City signs on its side wall.

LEFT
2nd

Shoney's
RESTAURANT
Home of the
BIG BOY
TRY OUR NEW
PHILLY CHEESE
STEAK SANDWICH

RAMADA INN

OPPOSITE: The chain of Shoney's restaurants did not begin in Tennessee but eventually ended up under Nashville ownership. Long associated with the Big Boy trademark, Shoney's dropped that connection in 1983. This photo was taken on US 78 in Memphis at dawn on a June morning in 1984, when the company had not yet gotten around to removing all the Big Boy signage. In the distance, note a neon Ramada Inn sign still glowing from the previous night and the Pizza Inn sign with its revolving chef.

ABOVE: Nashville artist John Baeder was able to capture this melancholy scene of multiple discarded Shoney's Big Boys awaiting their fate. Since the trademark legally belonged to the Marriott Corporation, Big Boy's parent company, most likely these were shuttled off to serve at other non-Shoney's locations across the country. *John Baeder collection.*

15¢
BURGER CHEF
HAMBURGERS
SHAKES

OPPOSITE: A craze for fifteen-cent hamburgers spawned many fast-food chains, including Burger Chef. It was long gone by the time this remarkably well-preserved sign was photographed on US 31 in Columbia in 1991. No trace of a building remained, only this sign, its neon chef and "15 cent" bulbs intact, standing in an overgrown, weedy lot.

ABOVE: There are, however, some surviving examples of former Burger Chef buildings. This one, as seen on US 11 in Cleveland in 2009, had simply changed its name to "The Chef" and retained Burger Chef's distinctive architecture with its trademark kite-shaped appendages.

BROOKS SHAW & SONS
OLD COUNTRY STORE
For a Barrel of old time fun, visit the Old Country Store—Jackson, Tennessee

SHELL
CRACKER BARREL
OLD COUNTRY STORE

OPPOSITE, TOP: This "Old Country Store" at Jackson became the model for a chain. Businessman Dan Evins cited it as his inspiration for the combination restaurant/gift shop that would become Cracker Barrel. As for this original, today it serves as the centerpiece of Jackson's Casey Jones Village mini–theme park and still serves up grub amid a re-created general store setting.

OPPOSITE, BOTTOM: Dan Evins opened his first Cracker Barrel at Lebanon in 1969. This is another of the early locations as it appeared in Manchester. Forgotten today by almost everyone is that the early Cracker Barrels sold gas along with meals and gift shop items. Also, note the dimensional barrel along the roofline instead of the more familiar signage.

ABOVE: It seems that either Jackson's Old Country Store or the emerging Cracker Barrel chain, or both, inspired others. The Bean Pot Restaurant at Crossville fit firmly into that same mold, combining food with gifts and antiques.

The Po Folks chain began in South Carolina in 1975, and for a while it followed the same trajectory as Cracker Barrel. By the mid-1980s, Po Folks had locations in seventeen states (with five in the Nashville area, as detailed on this souvenir cardboard fan). But soon the company began to shrink and today is found almost exclusively in the Florida Panhandle.

OPPOSITE, TOP: Those above a certain age may remember when Kentucky Fried Chicken was merely a menu item at scores of independent restaurants and drive-ins. The Travelers Restaurant in Maryville was part of the Colonel's early crowd, as seen here in 1960.

OPPOSITE, MIDDLE: By the mid-1960s, KFC had progressed to its own buildings (sometimes with indoor seating, sometimes not), distinguished from the roadside landscape by their pointed red-and-white-striped roofs topped with Colonel Sanders weathervanes. Of course, the sign with its flashing yellow arrow and rotating bucket did its part, too.

OPPOSITE, BOTTOM: Former KFC buildings are easy to recognize even when converted to other uses. This unusually tall, steep example in Elizabethton was still in business as a restaurant in 2016. Note that it sits next door to a former Pure gas station, with the *P* logo visible on its chimney.

Travelers
RESTAURANT
Kentucky Fried Chicken
EAT IN YOUR CAR

Kentucky Fried Chicken
COLONEL SANDERS RECIPE
Kentucky Fried Chicken
Kentucky Fried Chicken
"it's finger lickin' good."
OPEN
DINE IN
CARRY OUT
SERVICE
ICE
ICE

Nanny's
RESTAURANT

Minnie Pearl's
CHICKEN
See Minnie Pearl
in Person
at our
Grand Opening

Minnie Pearl's
ROAST BEEF

Minnie Pearl's Chicken

OPPOSITE, TOP LEFT & BOTTOM: In the late 1960s, celebrities ranging from Mahalia Jackson to Yogi Bear licensed their names to competing fried chicken chains. Minnie Pearl, of Opry fame, said "how-deee" to the concept. It was through no fault of Minnie's that the company fried in its own grease within a few years, mainly because its officials had no prior experience in the fast-food industry. *Al Coleman collection; John Baeder collection.*

OPPOSITE, TOP RIGHT: Minnie's fried chicken chain was already tottering on its drumsticks when its leaders rather unwisely decided to start a companion roast beef chain. Colonel Sanders had briefly dabbled in roast beef, so why not? The extinction of both chains may answer that question.

ABOVE: Another late-1960s entry into the chicken run was Chicken Chef. Like most, it got up to crow with the dawn but quickly went to roost when sundown—that is, financial downturns—came. Today, its sole remaining location is in McMinnville, looking just as it did nearly fifty years ago.

Long before "fried" became a somewhat taboo word among restaurants, Broasted Chicken had become a popular menu item for independent restaurants, just as KFC had once been. Bucky's in Columbia was one that boasted its broasted product with this top-hatted mascot. *Debra Jane Seltzer collection*.

OPPOSITE: Drive-ins offered a completely different type of culture than did Minnie Pearl's Chicken or Cracker Barrel. One of their most common emblems, as seen at this example in Seymour, was a cone, usually tilted, with a heapin' helpin' of soft-serve ice cream with a curl on top. As for the claim of "good food"—as Don Knotts said, "I'd rather eat good food than bad food any day." *John Margolies collection*.

Pixie
DRIVE-IN
GOOD FOOD

TOP: The date and location of this drive-in are unknown, but those who were a part of the era may remember the Hum-Dinger brand of milkshakes and their diagonally striped cups. This place employed some creative sign maker to re-create that design in neon. *Rock City collection.*

BOTTOM: There's that swirly ice-cream cone again, although it must be admitted that it appears that evil times hath befallen the derelict Dairy King in Nashville. Perhaps he lost a divorce settlement with his wife, the Dairy Queen. *Debra Jane Seltzer collection.*

OPPOSITE: Meanwhile, in Brownsville, the Kream Kastle kombined—er, combined—the cone with a curl on top with a neon porker that looked like what might have happened if Porky Pig and the Piggly Wiggly mascot had produced offspring. Numerous roadside photographers discovered and documented this sign from the late 1970s into the early 2000s, but apparently it has melted away like ice cream in July. *John Margolies collection.*

KREAM KASTLE
Coca-Cola
DRINK Coca-Cola

Knoxville's Hi-Boy, "a meal in one," sounds like it was trying hard to copy the double decker Big Boy hamburger. (For that matter, so was the Big Mac, but that's another story.) Note the neon carhop bearing goodies atop the sign, almost rusted into unrecognition. *John Margolies collection*.

We cannot neglect to look in on the Great Smoky Mountains before leaving this chapter. The Apple Tree Inn was one of innumerable businesses in that area begun by former Sevier County football player Charles "Z" Buda. The Green Valley Restaurant could be found in Pigeon Forge, with plenty of its titular color in evidence in the signage.

The intersection of I-40 and State Highway 66, where traffic exits to begin its journey into Sevierville, Pigeon Forge and Gatlinburg, has certainly grown since this late-1970s aerial view. The red-roofed Cross Forks Restaurant was formerly a location in the Nickerson Farms chain, yet another offshoot of Stuckey's. Go ahead and enjoy the vintage Best Western sign, too, as motels will be the topic of our next chapter.

THREE

THE NATION'S INNKEEPER AND HIS FRIENDS

In our previous chapter, we mentioned that Tennessee had given the restaurant world the immensely popular Cracker Barrel chain. In the motel industry, Tennessee gained another star in its crown—literally—by introducing millions to "the Nation's Innkeeper," Holiday Inn, and its iconic sign composed of neon and flashing bulbs topped with a giant star that pulsated in the night.

But Holiday Inn was only a part of the story, albeit a big one. This is the longest chapter in the book, mainly because motel imagery has been so well documented. It was rare to find a motel, whether part of a chain or a local mom-and-pop operation, that did not issue postcards for its visitors to mail home to friends and family. The number of these postcards that have survived to become collectibles today proves just how popular that custom became.

Motel postcards also had something in common that perhaps was not so evident to their clientele. Especially in the days before color photography became common, it was standard practice for postcard companies to use a black-and-white image and then "colorize" it (to resurrect a 1980s term). This meant that the sign and building might not appear the same color in print that they were in reality. Postcard printers were also fond of having their artists improve on the setting, painting in trees where there were none or turning paved parking lots into verdant expanses of green grass.

With so many motel photos in the pile of prospective choices, the ones that made the final cut are only a representative sample. They are not always the most historic from a permanency perspective, but each has its reason for being here. Now, get a good night's sleep before we hit the road again.

Before motels (or automobiles, for that matter), there were the big downtown hotels. They relied on huge rooftop signs to stand out among other tall buildings. Several pages ago we had an aerial view that included Chattanooga's venerable Hotel Patten; here is another angle, this time showing not only its signage but also the crossroads of major U.S. highways leading to far-flung destinations.

OPPOSITE: Over in Memphis, the William Len Hotel somewhat unusually relied on a tall vertical sign on its corner—more like a movie theater than most other hotels. Opened in 1930, it still serves lodging purposes as a Residence Inn.

HOTEL
WILLIAM LEN
MEMPHIS
WM. LEN HOTEL
COFFEE SHOP
WM LEN HOTEL
MAIN and MONROE
MEMPHIS, TENNESSEE
ENTRANCE ON MONROE

Now we're back in Knoxville at the Hotel Arnold, with a truly impressive rooftop display. (The lettering may or may not have been that shade of red in real life.) Built as an apartment house in 1923, it was converted into a hotel in 1928 but closed for demolition in 1962.

Even smaller towns had their own downtown hotels, such as this one in Dyersburg. In case you're not up on your Tennessee history, native son Cordell Hull served as U.S. secretary of state during World War II. Having a hotel named for him would indicate that this one came along a bit later than the others we have seen. It currently serves as a bank.

The Read House
and
NEW MOTOR INN
FREE PARKING · TV · RADIO · MUSIC
POOL
ROCK CITY

J.C.HARBIN'S TOURIST COTTAGES
MEMPHIS, TENN.
U.S.51
SOUTH
Easy to find
J.C.HARBIN
Fine Food-Beautyrest Mattresses
Swimming Pool-Baths-Steam & Gas Heat
7A-H1821

OPPOSITE, TOP: How's this for a transition from one age to another? Chattanooga's Read House Hotel dates to 1872, but in 1960 it received an annex of sorts—a more modern "motor inn." As they say, class will out, and while the motor inn is no longer there, the original Read House continues to serve customers in elegant style. *Rock City collection*.

OPPOSITE, BOTTOM: Tourist cabins evolved in the early automobile era for those new road warriors who were not interested in fancy hotels and snooty desk clerks. South of Memphis, it looks like J.C. Harbin chose to use himself as the sign for his cottages, at least on his elaborate postcards.

ABOVE: Soon, "courts" became a popular part of the name for roadside lodging. This example was discovered in Blaine many years ago. It still bore a remnant of the hotel era in its neon depiction of a bellboy with an animated arm pointing the way into the premises. *John Margolies collection*.

It is unfortunate that we do not know just where this was located. As we have seen, neon (and later, plastic) was the first choice for motel signage, but some anonymous artist certainly must have worked overtime creating this painted masterpiece. *Rock City collection.*

OPPOSITE, TOP: Imagine how eye-catching that entrance arch sign would have been to drivers on US 41. Of course, the complex it represented looks pretty cozy in this postcard, too. *Al Coleman collection.*

OPPOSITE, MIDDLE & BOTTOM: The Log Cabin Court in Pulaski must have been a welcome sight to weary travelers. Amazingly, in 1991, the miniature Abe Lincoln residences were still standing, although the property was for sale and there was no trace of the 1930s neon sign on its pole.

LEWIS MOTOR COURT
ONE MILE SOUTH OF TWIN TUBES ON U.S. 41
CHATTANOOGA, TENN.
LEWIS MOTOR COURT

LOG CABIN COURT - PULASKI, TENN.

FOR SALE

Lookout
MTN.
TOURIST
LODGE
COLOR TV & POOL

Approved
MEMBER
AMERICAN
MOTEL
ASSOCIATION

OPPOSITE: Now, here's a piece of neon artwork that is worth looking out for, especially on the slopes of Lookout Mountain. This view dates from around 1977, when photographer John Margolies was making his way across the southern states to see what sort of roadside relics still existed. *John Margolies collection.*

ABOVE: Sadly, this is what the Lookout Tourist Lodge had become by 2008. It is unlikely that the neon will ever be restored to anything resembling its original appearance. And, as you can see, the rest of the property was quickly following the sign's chieftain into history.

AIR
CONDITIONED
VACANCY
Anderson
MOTEL
RESTAURANT

RESTAURANT
TENNESSEE
MOTEL
POOL-FREE TV
RESTAURANT
VACANCY

OPPOSITE, TOP: There is so much to enjoy in this view of the Anderson Motel at Murfreesboro that it's hard to know where to begin. That sign with its sweeping arrow is a good start, but note the Coca-Cola "button" sign at the far left-hand side, and in the very center, a classic Esso service station with only the back of its rooftop sign visible. The lady in pink must have worked in the Anderson restaurant, where the postcard gives the expected specialties as "steaks, country ham, fried chicken and pork chops." Yummy yum yum! *Al Coleman collection.*

OPPOSITE, BOTTOM: Earlier we saw an example of the multiple Tennessean Restaurants, but here we have a Tennessee Motel whose location is unknown—except that we don't have to guess what state hosted it.

ABOVE: Well, if you're looking for a place for a long sleep, why not ask an expert? The Rip Van Winkle Motel on US 51 at Millington certainly took its name from the master of the topic. The only thing more fitting would have been to see people bowling at tenpins on the lawn. *Al Coleman collection.*

The Lynmac, at the southwestern city limits of Chattanooga, was one of the many motels that catered to those coming to see Rock City or gape at Ruby Falls. Besides the standard neon sign, the roof of the office had a multicolored neon spiral that added to its appeal. Nothing remains of the Lynmac today, and that green forest on the hill in back is now the location of a Walmart (what else?).

OPPOSITE, TOP: Some motels just squatted by the roadside, far from any tourist attractions or even a town. This rusting remnant of the Hickory Hill Motel still stands alongside US 70N east of Lebanon, but it is anyone's guess as to how long ago it and its café served any tourists driving that route.

OPPOSITE, BOTTOM: Let's face it, the style of this motel's signage and architecture would have been far more at home somewhere along US 41 in Florida than in the hills along that same highway in Tennessee. Making the Florida connection even stronger, the Monteagle Motel advertised that it was situated at "the highest point between Chicago and Miami." *Al Coleman collection.*

HICKORY HILL
MOTEL
Cafe
OFFICE

MOTEL
MONTEAGLE
Monteagle
RESTAURANT
COURT
VACANCY

T
V
KNOX
MOTEL
2 POOLS
✓KIDS
✓ADULTS

FREE
TV
KNOX
SWIMMING
POOLS
MOTEL
VACANCY
ENTRANCE
KNOX
MOTEL

OPPOSITE: These two views give us an inside peek into roadside evolution, this time in Knoxville. Neither has a date on it, but it is easy to see how the red vertical sign came to be replaced by the flashier and more eye-catching sign of the second card. The original vertical sign, however, can still be seen in the inset photo of the pool.

ABOVE: Another example of roadside metamorphosis over the years begins with this homey view of Lockmiller's Motel, which was located on US 41 just a few blocks closer to Lookout Mountain than the Lynmac we saw earlier.

The former Lockmiller's was probably at its lowest point in 2008, when the original sign was suffering from neglect under its then-current Mountain View Motel nomenclature. Believe it or not, the second photo was made only one year later, when the same sign proclaimed its new name as Chattanooga Inn and Suites. It wholeheartedly embraced its position as a classic 1940s cabin court reborn to serve twenty-first-century travelers.

Motels named after U.S. presidents? The Polk Motel in Columbia had a legitimate right, since the burg was proud of being the hometown of James K. Polk. The Eisenhower Motor Court in Newport might not have had any relationship to the 1950s chief executive at all; the sign certainly looks like it might have preceded Dwight D.'s stay in the White House. *Debra Jane Seltzer collection; John Margolies collection.*

TOP: This towering Tannenbaum was a landmark on I-75 at Caryville for many years. The motel itself was noted for celebrating Christmas all year long. When this photo was made in 2010, it was already closed, and the property no longer provided any holiday cheer.

BOTTOM: Shot through the dusty glass front door, this depressing photo shows the complete wreckage inside the former lobby of the Christmas Inn. In case you can't tell, those are hundreds of travel brochures and postcards ripped from their racks and piled on the floor—a gruesome and nightmarish sight for anyone who collects such memorabilia.

OPPOSITE: These two signs stood in Maryville in 2010, but neither exists today (although their motels do). Being named after the highway passing by its front lawn was fine and dandy for the 411 Motel; the Mountain View stretched things a little further. It was still several miles to the border of the Great Smoky Mountains National Park, but as the motel's name suggested, one could certainly view the mountains from there—just a long way off.

411 MOTEL
NO VACANCY
411 MOTEL
POOL
COLOR TV
KITCHENETTES

Mountain View
MOTEL
OPEN ALL YEAR
VISA

McAFEE'S
COURT

BILMAR
motor inn
YES
COLOR TV
PHONES
QUEEN BEDS

OPPOSITE, TOP: Once those tourists arrived in the Smokies proper, they were greeted by other lodging choices. McAfee's Court dated to the days when tiny Pigeon Forge bragged that the community had ten motels, the combined rooms of which could accommodate 250 people.

OPPOSITE, BOTTOM: If you will, please stop for a moment to savor all the delicious signage in this single 1970s view of the Bilmar Motor Inn in Pigeon Forge. You can probably make out the McAfee's sign from the previous photo just over the Bilmar's roofline, but across the street is the entrance sign for theme park Goldrush Junction. And the Cross Ties Restaurant? It is now the ticket office for Goldrush's present-day identity, a little place called Dollywood.

ABOVE: In 1952, Memphis businessman Kemmons Wilson set out to build a nationwide motel chain that would provide clean, comfortable and, most of all, dependable lodging. His first unit was located on Memphis's Summer Avenue. Inspired by the 1942 Bing Crosby movie of the same name, he called it Holiday Inn.

Holiday Inn
Holiday Inn
HOTEL
COURTS

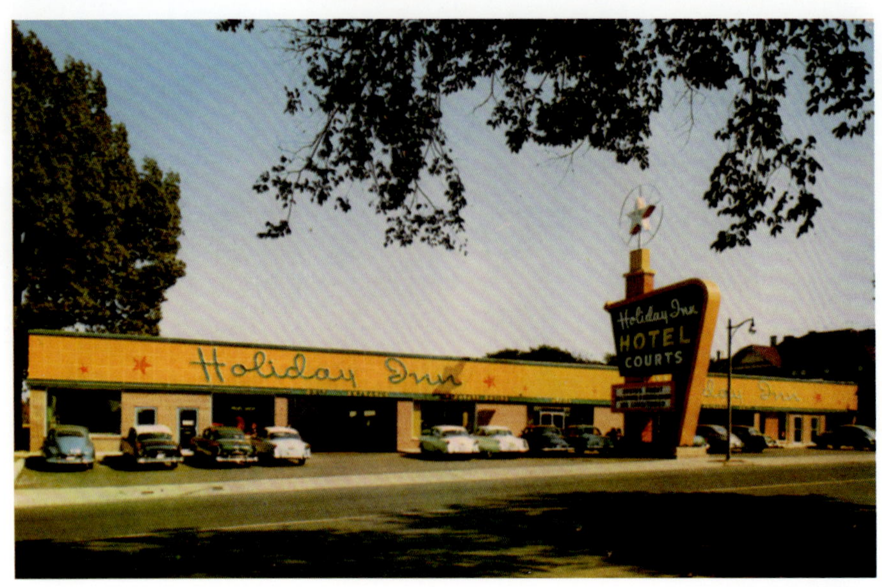

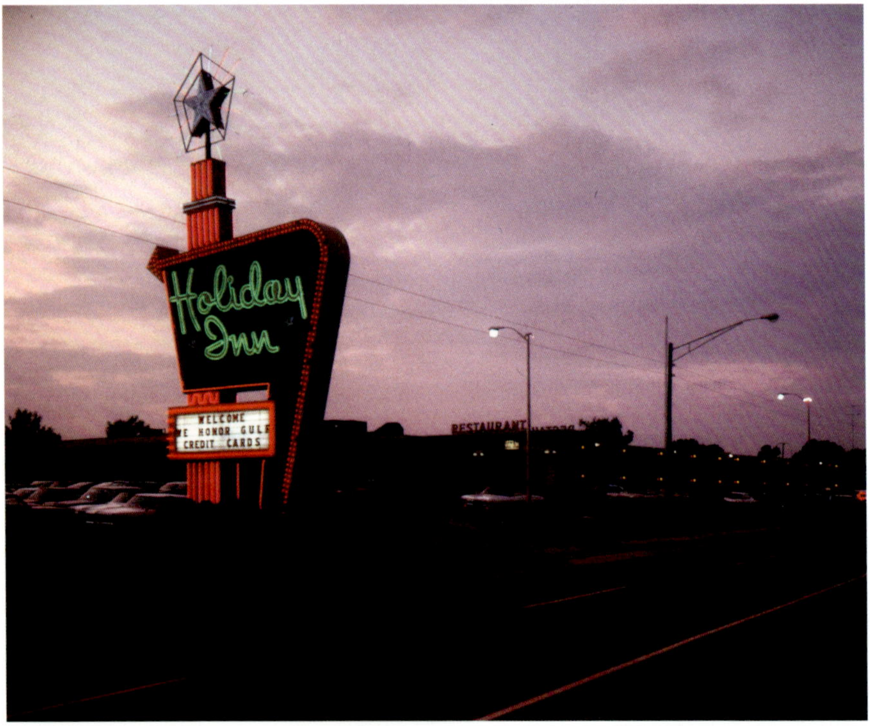

Holiday Inn
WELCOME
WE HONOR GULF
CREDIT CARDS
RESTAURANT

OPPOSITE, TOP: Beginning with that first location, Holiday Inn's most recognizable feature stood by the side of the road and was modestly known as the "Great Sign." This is an early example, also in Memphis, when the Great Sign still needed the additional explanation of "Hotel Courts" for those who were unfamiliar with the emerging chain.

OPPOSITE, BOTTOM: As seen here in Cleveland in the late 1960s, the Great Sign was a welcome nighttime sight to weary travelers. Some figures: each sign was 43 feet tall and had 836 feet of neon tubing and 426 incandescent bulbs. Each sign cost $35,000 to build, not counting electrical bills and maintenance costs. But any family who had been on the road for twelve hours and was looking for a place to crash for the night would have argued that the money spent was well worth it.

ABOVE: One requirement of any Holiday Inn was that it had to have its own restaurant, often heralded by another sign above the portico. The various Holiday Inn Restaurants developed such a reputation for quality food that people who were not even staying at the motel would make dinner plans to eat there.

Holiday Inn
Nashville
TENNESSEE

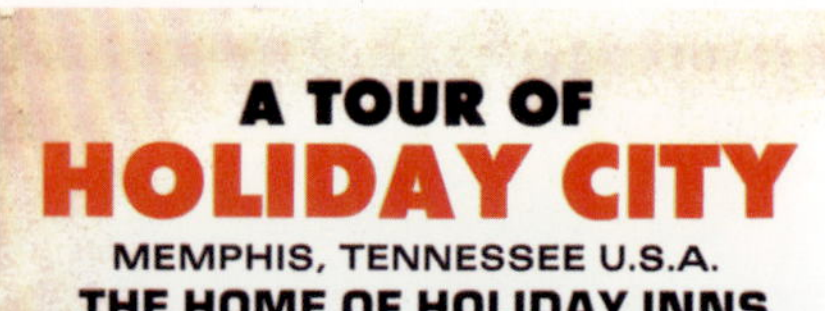
A TOUR OF
HOLIDAY CITY
MEMPHIS, TENNESSEE U.S.A.
THE HOME OF HOLIDAY INNS

Holiday Inn
OF AMERICA
THE
WORLDS
INNKEEPER
NOTE: This brochure is available in English, French, German, Spanish, Italian and Japanese. When ordering extra copies, please specify language desired.

HOLIDAY CITY COMPLEX

1. Holiday Inn - Southeast
2. Executive Building
3. Plaza Building
4. Holiday Manufacturing
5. Holiday Inn Dinner Theatre
6. Institutional Mart of America
7. General Data & Holidex Computers
8. Gulf Station
9. First National Bank
10. National Bank of Commerce
11. Union Planters National Bank
12. Holiday Press
13. Holiday Inn Manufacturing & Warehouse Facilities

OPPOSITE, LEFT: Okay, perhaps this staged photo is a bit corny, but the Nashville Holiday Inns came up with a perfect image to represent that musical city's lure for songwriters and performers. Unfortunately, the days of someone such as this young man showing up unannounced at the Opry and being put on the air were already long gone by the time of this circa 1972 brochure.

OPPOSITE, RIGHT: After spending many years known as the Nation's Innkeeper, Holiday Inn eventually went global and became the World's Innkeeper. Its international headquarters were situated on Lamar Avenue in Memphis, where US 78 entered the city from the southeast.

ABOVE: Holiday City was truly a city all its own, with everything needed to run Holiday Inn's worldwide empire. But it was not to last. Today, the former Holiday City, as well as the area of Lamar Avenue it largely supported, is a complex of mostly abandoned and derelict buildings. The Great Sign was phased out in 1983–84 to make way for cheaper plastic signage. Traveling at night hasn't been the same since.

Vacation
MOTOR
HOTEL
AUCTION
THUR. APRIL 22nd 10 AM
CLARKSVILLE LANDMARK PROPERTY
APPROXIMATELY 3.25 ACRES ZONED C-2
40,000 DAILY TRAFFIC COUNTS
AUCTION TEAM
The Prudential

OPPOSITE: As the song goes, "Something's happenin' here, and what it is ain't exactly clear." Many people have discovered this sign in Clarksville and assumed it is the remnant of a Great Sign. However, Holiday Inn never had a location there, and the company was extremely thorough in making sure no Great Signs were left to exist outside of certain museums. So, the Vacation Motor Hotel will have to remain the most mysterious vacation destination of all. *Debra Jane Seltzer collection.*

ABOVE: Only two years after Holiday Inn began, Howard Johnson's started adding motels to some of its existing restaurants. Eventually, the tail began to wag the hot dog, as the Motor Lodges came to totally replace the restaurants as a brand name. Yes, this sight in downtown Chattanooga was just as spectacular as it appears in this postcard, with a rooftop sign that could not be ignored.

The Motor Lodges' signs abstracted the Howard Johnson's logo into geometric shapes reminiscent of the restaurants' famed orange roofs and aqua-colored spires. But as the years have gone by, even that tenuous connection to their origins has been lost. This brochure was somewhat unusual in presenting a bikini model by the pool at night rather than working on her suntan.

OPPOSITE, TOP: A largely forgotten motel chain was Alamo Plaza, based (where else?) in Texas. True to its name, the company's buildings were miniature replicas of the famed San Antonio historical site. This one was still operating in Memphis in the 1970s, with signage that must have blazed in the night. *John Margolies collection.*

OPPOSITE, BOTTOM: Quality Courts was initially not so much a motel chain as a co-op deal by which member motels could reap the benefits of a familiar logo that assured travelers of their reputation. For example, this Quality Court was in Franklin but still bore the name of Town Motel underneath the sunburst sign.

ALAMO PLAZA
WELCOME
ALAMO PLAZA
Motel
MOTEL
DRIVE-IN
BE ALERT
SPEED LIMIT
35

QUALITY
COURTS
UNITED INC.
POOL TV PHONES
TOWN
MOTEL
AAA

This enormous Quality Court sat at the eastern end of the I-55 bridge (formerly the 1940s US 70 bridge) connecting Arkansas and Tennessee. Besides the sunburst logo, this brochure gives a great view of the multitude of directional signs that greeted those entering the Memphis city limits.

OPPOSITE: Best Western was a co-op similar to Quality Courts, in which the company logo would be added to the name of the motel. As seen in this example from the Nashville suburbs, the Best Western sign was pretty flashy, with literal flashing bulbs making up its golden crown. Like the Howard Johnson's logo, the Best Western crown has today been abstracted into a graphic design no one could identify.

Best Western
Maxwell's Inn

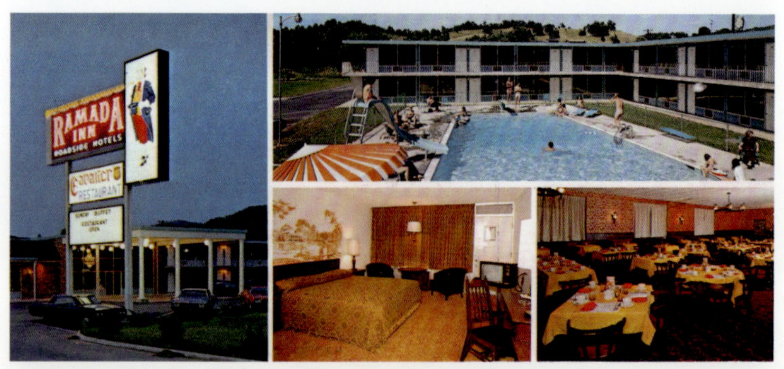

RAMADA INN
ROADSIDE HOTELS
Cavalier RESTAURANT

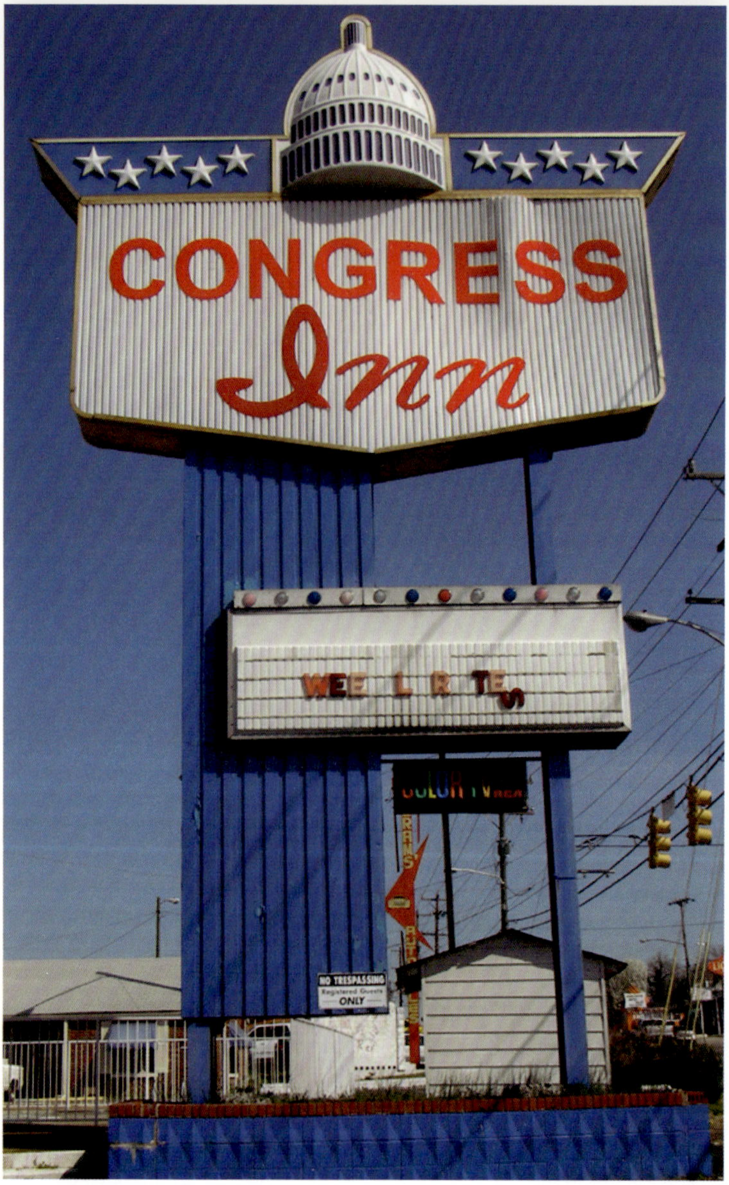
CONGRESS
Inn
NO TRESPASSING
Registered Guests
ONLY

OPPOSITE, TOP: And while we're on the subject of flashy signs, let's not forget the 1960s–'70s version of the Ramada Inn logo, with the name spelled out in hot-pink neon and a lighted panel picturing the company's innkeeper character, known as Uncle Ben. This one was in Pigeon Forge, but the same signage could be seen lighting up the night from coast to coast.

OPPOSITE, BOTTOM: There must be a joke somewhere about Congress being a good place to catch up on some sleep. That was not the inspiration for the Congress Inns, which began as yet another franchising co-op like Quality Courts and Best Western. The chain had been impeached by the 1980s, but this example of its sign was still hanging on in Nashville in 2007. *Debra Jane Seltzer collection.*

ABOVE: Albert Pick had been the brand name of a chain of big-city hotels, but in the 1950s it began to be applied to roadside motels as well. Obviously, the firm hoped to trade on the name's reputation for elegance. This particular Albert Pick Motel was in Nashville, but identical signs could be found in other Tennessee cities and elsewhere.

Nashville's Drake Motel and its giant sign dated to 1957. Its claim of "Stay Where the Stars Stay" might have had some validity in those days, but it's unlikely that one will find any Opry performers pickin' and grinnin' in front of their rooms there now. *Debra Jane Seltzer collection.*

OPPOSITE: There was probably little chance of encountering Roy Acuff at either of the two Fiddlers Inns locations in Nashville, but at least they had a logical tie-in with the region. Their signs were perhaps a bit disappointing to those who expected a little something more.

Fiddlers Inns
NASHVILLE, TENNESSEE
FIDDLERS MOTEL
CAMPGROUND REGISTRATION HERE
Briley Parkway at McGavock Pike and Music Valley Drive
NORTH (615) 885-1440
RESTAURANT
FIDDLERS · INN
FIDDLER'S INN
SOUTH
RESTAURANT · POOL · COLOR TV
Interstate 40 at Briley Parkway
SOUTH (615) 367-9202
COMFORT & LUXURY AT BUDGET PRICES
CALL FOR RESERVATIONS

Family
Inns
OF AMERICA
$12 77
UP
RESTAURANT
LOUNGE

OPPOSITE: Family Inns of America could just as well have been called Family Inns of the Smokies, since practically all of its locations were (and still are) in that part of Tennessee, including this one at Newport. We're glad the Howard Johnson's bikini model is finally managing to soak up some rays by their pool.

ABOVE: When the Chattanooga Choo-Choo complex was developed around the former railroad terminal station in 1973, this animated train sign was installed on the roof and is still there. The associated hotel company has changed a few times since then; note that at this particular juncture it bore the logo of the Hilton Hotels chain.

There were those who preferred camping to being cooped up in a motel room. For them, there were facilities such as the Camp'n Aire Resorts. Such places were experiencing a growth spurt in the late 1960s, including the Yogi Bear's Jellystone Park campgrounds and Stuckey's "CamPark" properties. This Camp'n Aire seems to be suggesting that TraveLodge's longstanding Sleepy Bear mascot might find the top of its sign more comfortable than a bed.

FOUR

HAPPY MOTORING

Okay, kiddies, just gather 'round my rocking chair and listen while I tell you about how things were in the olden days. Would you believe there was a time when people didn't use the price of gas as their main reason for choosing where to fill up? Would you believe there was a time when gas was so cheap that it really didn't matter where you bought it? Would you believe President Richard Nixon assured the nation that no American would ever have to pay a dollar for a gallon of gas? You'd better believe it!

Until the early 1970s, the price of a gallon of gasoline was negligible, so the major oil companies relied on building brand loyalty among their customers—just as Holiday Inn or Howard Johnson's or Kentucky Fried Chicken did. They often did this by offering premiums to entice drivers, or the children in the back seat (not wearing seat belts, of course), to stop under their rotating signage. Sinclair had its green dinosaur trademark, which could be adapted into inflatable beach toys, T-shirts, molded wax figures and other items. Gulf sponsored the weekly Disney TV show and promoted that connection with Disney records, place mats, magazines and other merry merchandise.

In this chapter, we will see some familiar old logos, such as the oval that represented the Humble Oil Company as it made its way through various brand names: Esso, Enco and, finally, Exxon. There will also be some that are nearly forgotten today, victims of mergers that erased them from the roadside landscape—sometimes temporarily, sometimes permanently. All had their loyal customers, some of whom just might have been you.

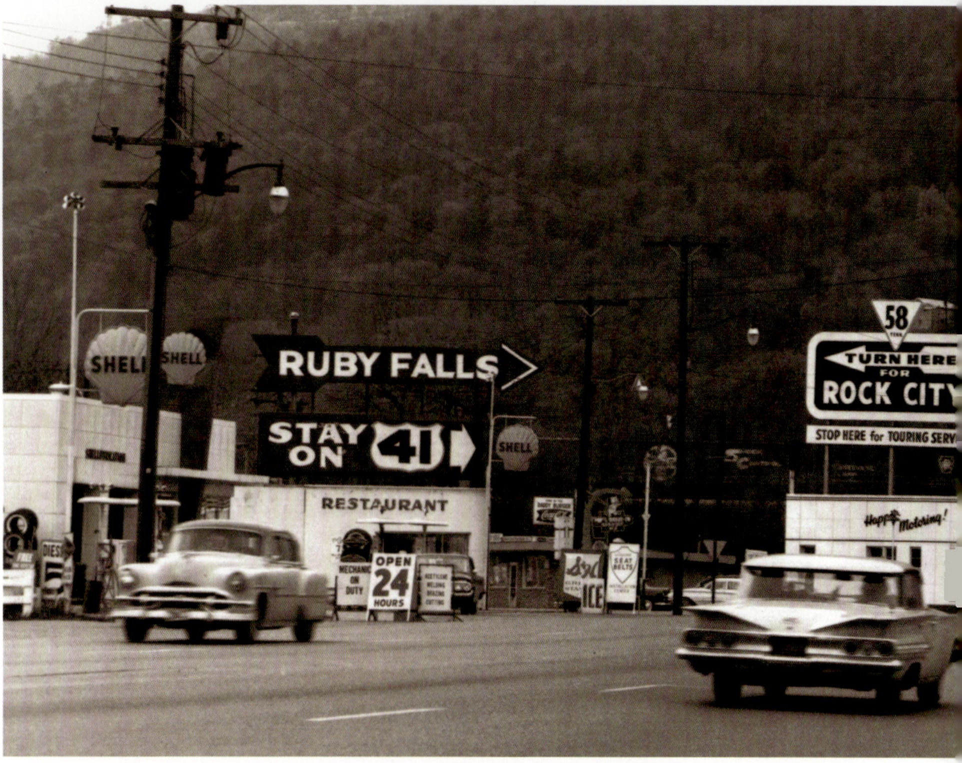
SHELL
SHELL
RUBY FALLS
STAY ON 41
SHELL
RESTAURANT
MECHANIC ON DUTY
OPEN 24 HOURS
SEAT BELTS
ICE
58
TURN HERE FOR ROCK CITY
STOP HERE for TOURING SERV
Happy Motoring!

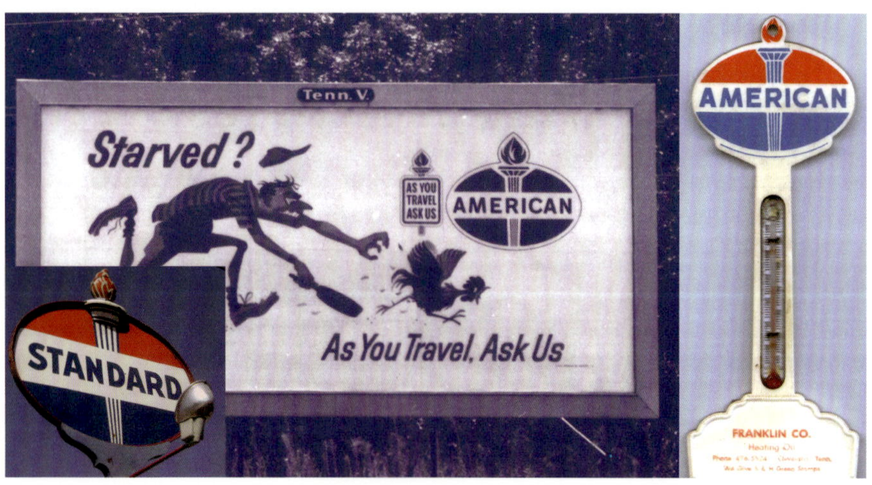

Tenn. V.
Starved?
AS YOU TRAVEL ASK US
AMERICAN
As You Travel, Ask Us
STANDARD
AMERICAN
FRANKLIN CO.
Heating Oil

ABOVE: This incredible panorama shows the busy intersection of US 11/US 41 in Chattanooga with State Highway 58, which climbed the slopes of Lookout Mountain en route to Rock City and the other sights. Obviously, the major oil companies thought that junction would be a good place for drivers to stop and fill up before continuing their trip, as a good number of them can be seen from this angle. Still other facilities did not necessarily make it into this view. *Rock City collection.*

OPPOSITE: The "torch and oval" could be found representing various brand names in different parts of the country, but in the 1960s it came to be associated with the American logo. As seen in the inset photo, from its days as a logo for Standard Oil, some of the signs were two-dimensional except for the lighted glass torch at the top. The thermometer, in case you can't read the stamp on the base, was given out by a station in Cleveland.

PEPSI
PEPSI
AMERICAN

SHELL
CLINCH
LOOKOUT

OPPOSITE, TOP: A later version of the American sign, illuminated by spotlights, could be found in Loretta Lynn's re-created small town at Hurricane Mills. Although we are primarily talking about gas stations here, those 1960s Pepsi "bottle cap" metal signs are worth a glance, too.

OPPOSITE, BOTTOM: Today, the Shell Oil logo, like so many others, has been reduced to an almost abstract rendition, without even the name to identify it. In this image, we can see the Shell shell in its earlier, more literal form. And as an added incentive to fill up, it seems the Clinch Mountain Lookout restaurant and gas station at Thorn Hill also gave S&H Green Stamps.

ABOVE: The Esso brand is so long gone that only older folks will remember it. The unusual name was originally an abbreviation for Standard Oil (S.O.), but by the time a station in Lebanon was giving away these 1956 calendars, more people associated Esso with its "Happy Motoring!" slogan that brightened up each of its buildings.

Here's a 1967 look at that Esso station we saw in the panoramic view of the base of Lookout Mountain. It certainly appears that this was one of the largest renditions of that logo to be found. Within a couple of years, Esso would be replaced by Enco, and in the early 1970s, both brands became Exxon. *Rock City collection*.

Esso was famous for its "Put a Tiger in Your Tank" ad campaign, with a cartoon feline appearing on signage and premiums of all stripes. There were even larger-than-life statues of the friendly beast; this one turned up at a Sevierville antiques store in 2015.

Sinclair
KODAK
3 ROL
DINO
28.9

Sinclair Gasoline
WITH
NICKEL
COMPOUND
MORE MILES PER DOLLAR!
ACO
SINCLAIR

OPPOSITE, TOP: Whereas Esso/Enco/Exxon used a tiger, Sinclair's animal emblem was a green dinosaur, meant to represent the age of its crude oil reserves. This Sinclair station at Lookout Mountain was a rather basic affair with no unusual architecture. But look closely, and you will see numerous examples of now highly prized collectible souvenirs hanging around its windows. *Rock City collection.*

OPPOSITE, BOTTOM: Unemployed Sinclair dinosaur statues can still be found in front of a wide-ranging variety of businesses. Sinclair never went completely extinct, but in the early 1970s, its stations east of the Mississippi River switched to the Atlantic Richfield (Arco) brand. Recently, Sinclair has been making an attempted comeback in the eastern half of the country, so maybe we will be able to visit with Dino again someday soon.

ABOVE: The Gulf stations stayed away from pictorial trademarks and instead urged drivers to "stop at the sign of the orange disk." This 1962 photo came shortly before the Gulf sign changed from the one seen here to another orange disk with a white space in the middle. Note the distinctive shape of Lookout Mountain looming in the background. *Rock City collection.*

CITIES
SERVICE

OPPOSITE: What, you say you don't remember the green and white Cities Service signs? Maybe that's because in 1965 the company shorted its name to Citgo, with a red and orange triangle as its logo. During the Cities Service days, it entered the animal mascot derby with its character Eager Beaver, who appeared in giveaway comic books and animated TV spots. *Rock City collection.*

TOP: Speaking of derbys, here's a gas station sign that was far less common. Derby Oil was primarily represented in the Midwest, but John Margolies found this example along Highway 45E in Milan around 1980. *John Margolies collection.*

BOTTOM: The Spur gas stations were originally headquartered in Nashville but really expanded their territory after being purchased by Murphy Oil. This late-era Spur sign was spotted in 2019 at Shelton Lane Antiques in Manchester.

KAYO
29
30

USED CARS
CHEVROLET
CARS & TRUCKS

Ford
FORD
Dodge
Plymouth
MOTORS

OPPOSITE, TOP: Kayo might not be the most familiar name in gas stations, and it is not to be confused with the chocolate drink of the same name, which would likely do nothing in an internal combustion engine. However, Kayo Oil's roadside presence was dynamic. Those vertical fuel tanks painted with red-and-white candy cane stripes were real eye-catchers. At the extreme right side of this photo, note Kayo's Freddy Fast mascot character, who bore a slight resemblance to Speedy Alka-Seltzer. *Rock City collection.*

OPPOSITE, MIDDLE: While we're on the subject of automotive businesses, let's not forget that there were others besides gas stations—car dealerships, for example, without which the gas stations would have had no customers. Edd Roberts Chevrolet on US 70 in Sparta is known for its preservation of several vintage signs in its lot. *Debra Jane Seltzer collection.*

OPPOSITE, BOTTOM: This fading sign in Woodbury might not be noticeable at all when the foliage is in its summer glory, but the barren limbs of fall and winter reveal its presence each year. The dealership is designated as dating back to 1922, but research has failed to disclose how long it has been since it occupied this piece of property.

ABOVE: Yes, for decades Chattanooga had a dealership called Amos & Andy Buick. Contrary to what many people might have thought, it was not named after the famous radio serial—the owners were really named Amos and Andy Trotter. And of course, they had totally coincidentally received their names years before the radio program's 1928 debut. *Rock City collection.*

This appears to be one of the Phillips 66 cottage-style gas stations converted into a Nashville used-tire business, with a color scheme about as opposite Phillips' orange-and-black one as possible. Note the phone booth at far right, which is now just as historic a sight as the venues in the rest of the photos in this book. *John Margolies collection.*

OPPOSITE: With a franchise called Bonanza Homes, this chain of mobile-home dealerships must have taken pains to not infringe on the Bonanza Steakhouses or the characters from the TV show of the same name. There was not much left of this mustachioed cowpoke in Knoxville in the late 1970s, but at least no one could have mistaken him for Ben Cartwright—or Hoss or Little Joe. *John Margolies collection.*

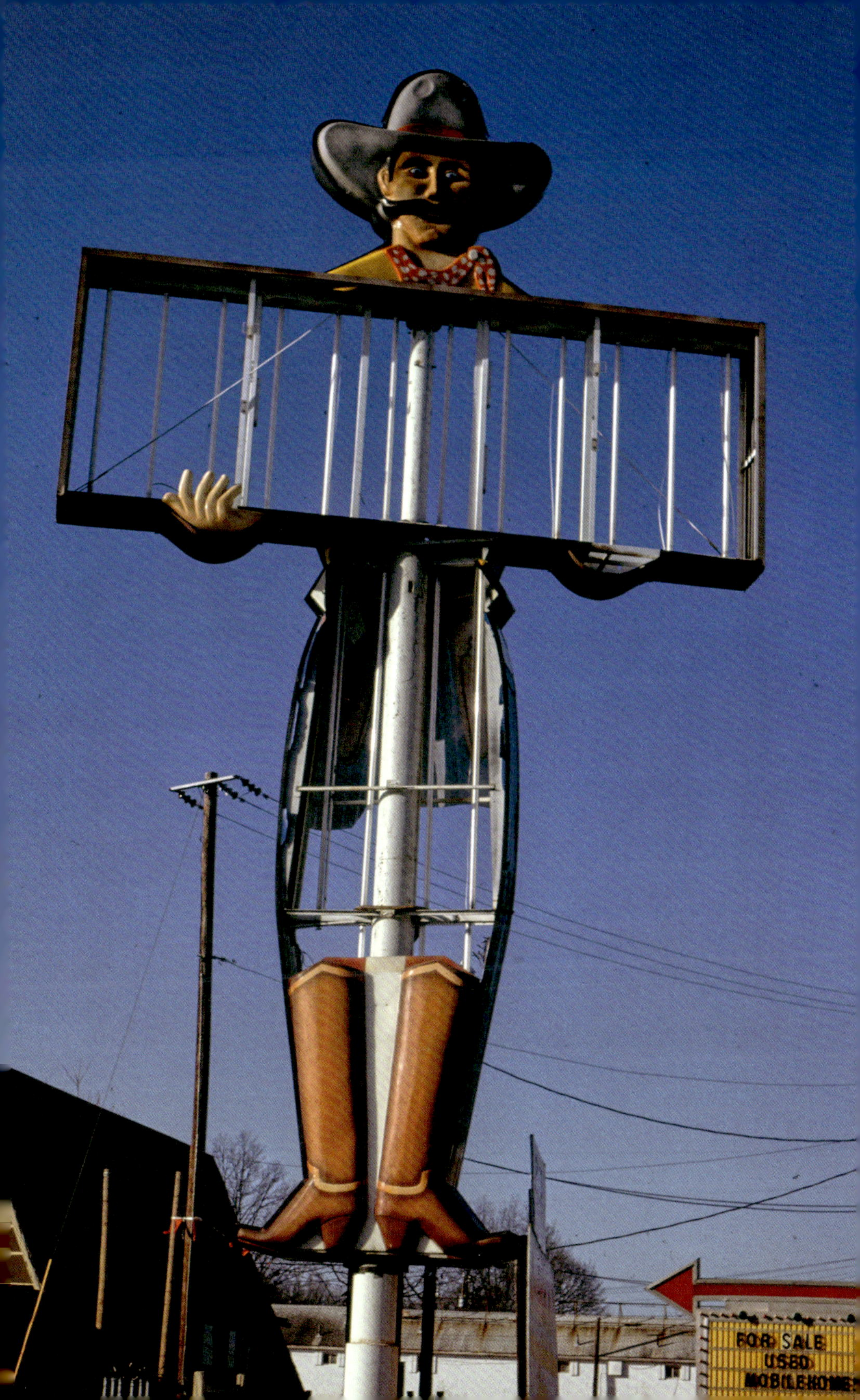
FOR SALE
USED
MOBILEHOMES

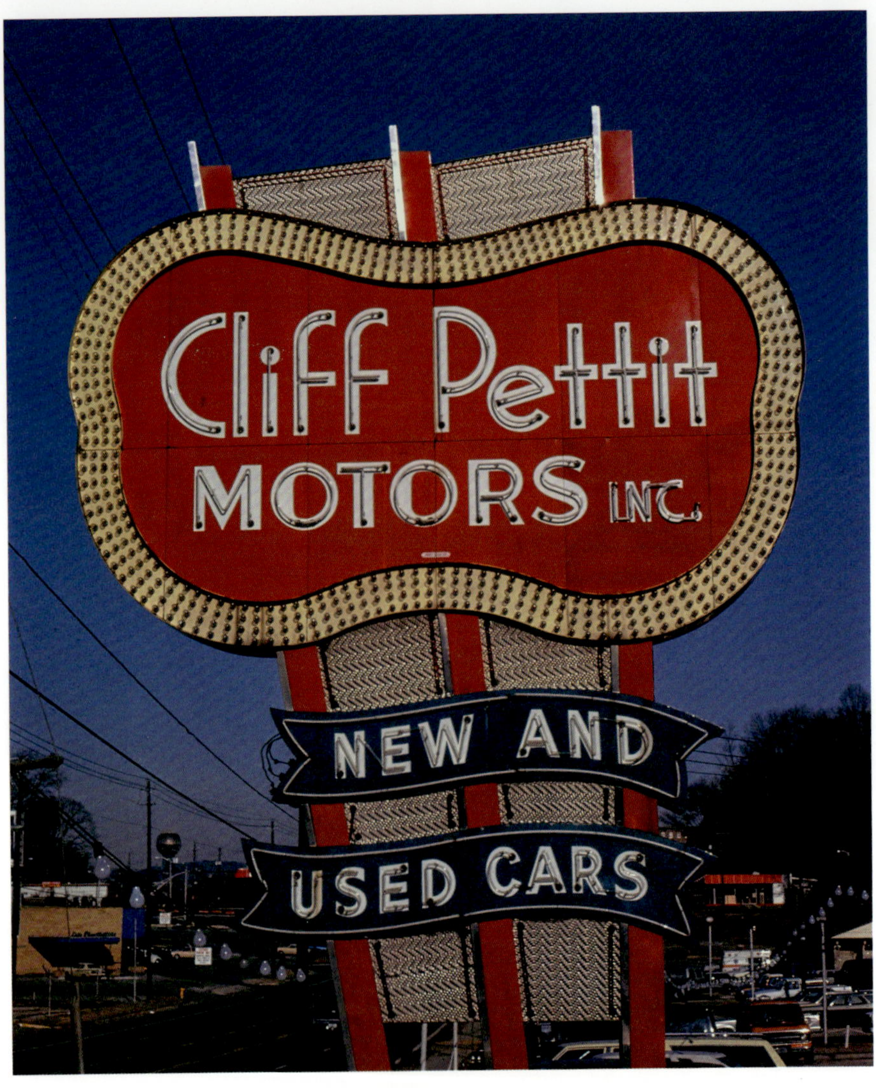

We don't have to guess at the location or approximate date photographer John Margolies captured this dealership's flashy sign. In the background on the left-hand side, note the Sunsphere, the emblem of the 1982 Knoxville World's Fair. *John Margolies collection.*

FIVE

ARE WE THERE YET? NO!

When it came to tourist attractions, Tennessee could not boast the sheer numbers that existed in Florida, but it was miles ahead of some of its neighbors, such as Alabama and Kentucky. Even at that, the vast majority of Tennessee's attractions were bunched together in two major locations: the Great Smoky Mountains, where tourists were as thick as molasses in January; and the area around Chattanooga and Lookout Mountain, which happened to be situated directly on several of the major tourist routes that led from the North and the Midwest toward the Sunshine State.

In this chapter, we will see plenty of representatives from both tourist centers, although it might seem that we have skimped somewhat on the Smokies. The main reason for that is the existence of my own previous books on the subject, *The Land of the Smokies: Great Mountain Memories* (2007), *Lost Attractions of Sevier County* (2011) and *Lost Attractions of the Smokies* (2020). Those made it more difficult to find material that had not already been covered, but there is a seemingly endless supply. Rock City has also been well represented in previous Hollis volumes, but its companions in the Lookout Mountain neighborhood have been less visible, so here they finally get due recognition.

That isn't to say that the rest of the state didn't jump into the tourism race with all four wheels spinning. It's just that outside of the aforementioned mountain areas, attractions seemed to be scattered along the major highways, where they could lure in tourists on their way to somewhere else. We will be visiting some of those in this chapter as well and seeing how their presence served to enliven what was often a long, boring drive.

NORTH CITY STATE 8
GLENDALE
TOURIST
COURT
BRICK COTTAGES
STEAM HEAT
CHATTANOOGA HARDWARE CO.
2615 BROAD ST.
CHATTANOOGA, TENN.
DE
DIAMOND EDGE TOOLS
U-HAVE-PASSED LOOKOUT MT.

Veteran's
GUIDE
SERVICE
WHERE TO GO
WHAT TO SEE
DRIVE IN
STOP
FOR DETAILS
LOOKOUT MT.
HEADQUARTERS
LOOKOUT
MTN.
GUIDES
LICENSED BY
STATE OF TENN.
COUNTY OF HAMILTON
CABINS
OFFICE ON HILL
CITY OF LOOKOUT MT.
CITY OF CHATTANOOGA
FOR TOURIST
THIS IS IT!
MOUNTAIN
GUIDES-DRIVERS
AND
HISTORIANS

OPPOSITE, TOP: Lookout Mountain had been a tourist destination since before the Civil War—before it had any attractions, even. This 1940s sign must have been directed at those who missed the right road. And briefly back to the topic of motels—that hand-lettered sign for Glendale Tourist Court looks like the facility might not have had all the amenities of a Holiday Inn or Howard Johnson's Motor Lodge. *Rock City collection.*

OPPOSITE, BOTTOM: The aforementioned Rock City histories give a more thorough explanation of the Lookout Mountain guides, which were mostly a pre–World War II phenomenon. For a fee, guides would take over tourists' cars and drive them to the various attractions. The problem came when the guides used questionable tactics—including outright lies about how dangerous the mountain highways were—in order to extort money from their vacationing victims. *Rock City collection.*

ABOVE: Once they reached Lookout Mountain's summit, either under their own power or with a guide at the wheel, most folks wanted to visit the site of the Civil War "Battle Above the Clouds." This 1937 postcard illustrated the museum and restaurant at the park's entrance, both of which obviously relied on lots of signage to get their message across.

After changing traffic patterns and beautification efforts eradicated many of the traditional Rock City barns, the Rock City birdhouse became their de facto replacement. This painted brick sign on Broad Street was meant to help the traffic flow; it's just too bad that the antiques store in its building had already gone out of business at the time of this 1991 photo.

OPPOSITE, TOP: This giant Broad Street billboard was widely touted as the "World's Biggest Birdhouse," and several nearby businesses advertised their locations in relation to its position—understandably, since it was more than easy to spot. *Rock City collection.*

OPPOSITE, BOTTOM: One of the most unusual publicity stunts took place in 1971, when Rock City made a big deal out of removing one—count 'em, *one*—of its billboards alongside US 41 at Guild and replacing it with a freshly planted evergreen tree, along with a plaque explaining its significance. It is not known whether the tree or the plaque still exist, as their specific location was not indicated. *Rock City collection.*

SEE
ROCK
CITY
LOOKOUT
MOUNTAIN
LEFT LANE
Dino's
PIZZA & PASTA
Italian Restaurant
LIVE MUSIC
BROADWAY
Home and Garden
Center

SEE SEVEN STATES
From
CITY
MOUNTAIN

TOP: Ruby Falls was often mentioned in the same breath as Rock City. Its opening actually predated that of Rock City by several years, and the two remained friendly rivals (at least most of the time) ever afterward. Ruby Falls devised its own unique advertising, such as perching this tractor trailer atop two supporting poles on I-24. *John Margolies collection.*

BOTTOM: Ruby Falls was also not above borrowing a page from Rock City's playbook. This gas station in Seymour sported one of Ruby Falls' own rooftop signs—much more colorful than the traditional white lettering/black background of the Rock City barns. *John Margolies collection.*

TOP: The Lookout Mountain Incline was not just an attraction; it remains a vital part of Chattanooga's public transit system. But it did depend on tourists to help defray the costs of operation, and in the 1950s and '60s, this neon sign showed them where to get off—or maybe on, depending on the direction they were traveling.

BOTTOM: This view of the Incline's lower station is interesting, because it shows a very short-lived attraction in the left-hand corner: Chattanooga's own Hall of Presidents Wax Museum, apparently on the second floor of a record store. In front, one of those ubiquitous Kay's Kastles ice-cream cones can also be glimpsed.

When people complained about the clutter of billboards and other signage along the nation's highways, this is what they meant. There are almost too many signs to count at the base of Lookout Mountain. But they must have made a colorful sight when they were all illuminated at night. *Rock City collection.*

OPPOSITE, TOP: This well-remembered attraction was in the same neighborhood as the sign clutter we just saw. As times changed, the Confederama name and theme smacked of a bygone era, and today most of its former exhibits can be found in historical context at the Battles for Chattanooga Museum. That exhibit occupies the same space as the Point Park restaurant and museum we saw a few pages ago.

OPPOSITE, BOTTOM: Crystal Cave, alternatively known as Crystal Cavern, advertised with these metal signs for miles around Chattanooga. This one was still clinging to a crumbling barn in 1992. Today, the signs are gone but Crystal Cave still exists as part of the Raccoon Mountain entertainment complex.

CONFEDERAMA

CRYSTAL CAVE
"CHATTANOOGA'S BEST ATTRACTION"
OR YOUR MONEY BACK

WONDER CAVE

WONDER CAVE

OPPOSITE, TOP: An even showier show cave was Wonder Cave, on US 41 at Monteagle. Somehow, this attraction managed to find a few barns that had escaped Rock City's painters. The location of this one is unknown (twelve miles to the cave being our only clue), but chances are that it disappeared many years ago. *Rock City collection.*

OPPOSITE, BOTTOM: Wonder Cave closed to the public for the first time in 1986, although it reopened for brief periods over the next ten years. As of August 2009, its fading entrance sign still stood next to US 41. As with most caves that were unable to survive in the world of commercial attractions, it now serves only professional spelunkers.

ABOVE: Now we move into the world of the Great Smoky Mountains, where Pigeon Forge's Hill-Billy Village was one of that town's first permanent attractions when it opened in 1954. Even after the venue closed in 2016, this billboard still staked out a spot along US 441, advertising a place tourists could no longer visit.

After staging live shows in several different Sevier County locations, comedian Archie Campbell moved into his own Hee Haw Village complex in Pigeon Forge in 1981. After Campbell's death in 1987, its heart was gone, but it managed to survive on borrowed time until 1996. The site is now home to the well-advertised Comedy Barn and the Frizzle Chicken Restaurant, with its cast of animatronic cluckers.

OPPOSITE: The Smoky Mountain Car Museum was another 1950s arrival in Pigeon Forge. Its collection of classic cars was a real crowd-pleaser until it put on the brakes around 2015. Comparing the vintage photo with the one from 2016, when the empty building sat awaiting its fate, shows that it went through some remodeling in those sixty years. By the end, its sign had been reduced to a banner stretched across the front.

Cars are restored to their original appearance—many are in good running order.

Located at Pigeon Forge, Tennessee on U.S. Highway 441 . . . Next to Fort Weare Game Park.

MAGIC
WORLD

Music Valley
WAX MUSEUM
of the Stars
WAX MUSEUM

OPPOSITE, TOP: Magic World was a small Pigeon Forge theme park owned by miniature-golf impresario Jim Sidwell (he was also responsible for Jolly Golf in Gatlinburg). Long before Magic World evolved into having its own logo, this rather basic corrugated plastic roadside sign did the job of attracting kids and parents. *Ruth Matthews collection.*

OPPOSITE, BOTTOM & LEFT: In the tourist biz, wax museums seem to come and go in a willy-nilly fashion (no relation to Willie Nelson). Nashville's Music Valley Wax Museum should have benefited from its proximity to Opryland, but maybe people just thought the building was a former Cracker Barrel that had fallen on hard times. As of this writing, the building was serving as a golf supply store.

Long after the embarrassing debacle of Minnie Pearl's Chicken, the beloved comedian opened her own museum near the Country Music Hall of Fame. Unfortunately, it did not last very long, but at least the structure and signage looked like something that might have been transplanted from the fictional version of Grinder's Switch.

OPPOSITE: Speaking of the Hall of Fame, the Car Collectors Hall of Fame made a rather blatant attempt to copy that more famous museum's façade, even though it was housed in something more closely resembling a warehouse. Neither the cars nor the ersatz entrance can be found there today.

CAR
COLLECTORS
HALL OF FAME
NASHVILLE
CAR COLLECTORS
HALL OF FAME

ONE HOUR
PHOTO
COUNTRY STORE
M M MELS
FINEST STORE
ON THE ROW
GUINNESS
HALL OF WORLD RECORDS

CONWAY
COUNTRY STORE
SHOP
RECORDS
FREE!
STAR
WILD WEST
SHIRT SHOP

OPPOSITE: In the same neighborhood just off Music Row, along Demonbreun Street, this string of businesses sought to cash in on as many country music stars' names as humanly possible. Both Mel Tillis and Conway Twitty had their own "country stores" (the latter with the Looney Tunes–inspired Twitty Bird on its sign), and of course we all expected to see Barbara Mandrell working behind the counter at her one-hour photo shop.

TOP: Lake Tansi Village still exists as a resort and residential development, but its cartoon Native Americans who beckoned from this giant sign have moved on to their Happy Hunting Grounds. The inset shows the resort's 1960s mascot, Miss Tansi.

BOTTOM: So, these aren't Burma-Shave signs, but they took the same advertising approach by spelling out their message in consecutive boards that could be read as cars sped past. They could be seen along US 70 leading to Pegram in the late 1970s or early '80s, but the name of the actual business they promoted is not visible. *John Margolies collection.*

If this were a book in our Lost Attractions series, we could not have included this photo, as the Davy Crockett Tavern Pioneer Museum is still king of the wild frontier in its home of Morristown. However, its present-day sign is considerably more sophisticated than this early version. A typesetter might question the validity of using all upper-case Gothic lettering for the "TAVERN" line, though.

SIX

AMOOZIN' BUT CONFOOZIN'

Admittedly, the line between "attractions" and "amusements" is a fine one, and here in our final chapter it might sometimes become almost invisible. There are some reasons for separating the two, although they are just about as arbitrary as they appear.

For example, let's take movie theaters, which have traditionally been known for their incredible signs and marquees. People definitely go to theaters for amusement, but they aren't necessarily tourist attractions. So, why include amusement parks in this section when they do attract tourists? Well, parks such as Nashville's Fair Park were there primarily for locals, whereas Opryland USA was a nationally advertised destination. It seemed most logical to lump them together, regardless of their intended audience.

Speaking of Opryland, it was home to one of the most historic Tennessee signs that was unavailable for this book. When the park opened in 1972, quite naturally one of its two railroad depots was named Grinder's Switch, after the fictional hometown of Minnie Pearl. Well, Grinder's Switch was indeed a real place, but merely a spur track in Hickman County. The L&N Railroad generously agreed to let Opryland have the sign from the real Grinder's Switch to use at its depot, but no reproducible photo of that sign could be located before press time. And oddly enough, when Opryland closed and the contents of the park were auctioned off, the Grinder's Switch sign was not a part of the inventory. It may be hanging in some collector's home to this day.

But even without the Grinder's Switch sign, there are plenty of other amusements to be seen here. If the choice sometimes seems a bit random, just keep in mind that phrase that was often used by the characters in Al Capp's *Li'l Abner* comic strip: "It's amoozin' an' confoozin'...kin yo' figger it out?"

POLK

OPPOSITE: We have already seen how Columbia saluted its local-boy-made-president James Polk with a motel named for him. This movie theater on US 31 opened a little over a century after Polk's death. Its closing date is more uncertain, but the sign was still in good shape when this 1991 photo was taken. The building has been serving as a mattress store for a number of years, with the only identifiable part of the sign being the neon spiral at the top.

ABOVE: One can only imagine how the towering pylon of Nashville's Belle Meade Theater must have looked to its first patrons in 1940. After its closure more than fifty years later, the businesses that took its place preserved the sign as part of the current complex known as Belle Meade Town Center. *Debra Jane Seltzer collection.*

In our first chapter, we saw some of the magnificent downtown movie palaces, but there were dozens of small neighborhood theaters as well. This one in Memphis, not surprisingly, was named after its location on Lamar Avenue (US 78) and has endured several decades of neglect since closing in the late 1970s. *Debra Jane Seltzer collection*.

OPPOSITE: This radio tower, billed as the tallest in the country, was bigger than any sign. It was the main reason WSM and the Grand Ole Opry were able to become nationally known in the late 1920s and throughout the 1930s, as WSM's clear-channel status and the sheer power of its signal reached into most of the lower forty-eight states. The tower can still be seen alongside I-65 in the Brentwood section of Nashville.

8—WSM—AMERICA'S TALLEST RADIO TOWER, 878 FEET, NASHVILLE, TENN.
5A-H430
323 FEET HIGHER THAN THE WASHINGTON MONUMENT

RADIO WMSR 1320
ANTIQUES
S&H
GREEN
STAMPS
STOP

SIR
GOONY
GOLF

OPPOSITE, TOP: Just as movie palaces had counterparts in small neighborhoods, so did WSM have its lower-wattage cousins in the radio world. WMSR was one of those, in Manchester. Like so many others, it had its call letters and frequency spelled out in neon along the roofline. The station is still operating, but its vintage sign was spotted in 2019 at Shelton Lane Antiques. It has since been purchased and returned to the family who founded the station.

OPPOSITE, BOTTOM: The chain of Sir Goony Golf courses began on Brainerd Road (US 11) in Chattanooga. The original is still there, even though its exact location has changed a few times. This version of its sign, with its goony alphabet blocks, has been replaced by its current appellation of Sir Goony's Family Fun Center. *John Margolies collection.*

ABOVE: At the other end of miniature-golf style was Putt Putt Golf, which discarded the giant concrete dinosaurs and other gimmicks of Sir Goony in favor of a more professionally challenging sporting experience. This unusual sign denoted the course on Airport Road in Gatlinburg, which was razed long ago. *John Margolies collection.*

Memphis's Skateland, with a roller skate that must have belonged to Mercury (to judge by its wings), was a local landmark for those wishing for an inexpensive date. This sign reportedly did not survive its final move into newer lodgings, and the winged skate flew away into the wild blue somewhere or other. *Vance Lauderdale collection.*

OPPOSITE: Any amusement place along the busy Pigeon Forge strip had to face the challenge of standing out among all the clutter. The Rebel Yell Raceway's solution was to erect its own Godzilla replica—graphically illustrating the idea of "go big or go home." *John Margolies collection.*

REBEL YELL
RACEWAY
BUMPER BOATS
MINI GOLF
LARGEST SELECTION T-SHIRTS
AIRBRUSHING
WELCOME
GROUP
DISCOUNTS

Nashville's Fair Park was fairly (ha, ha) typical of the local "kiddieland" amusement parks that sprang out of the ground to serve the ever-growing baby boom population. Its sign with Humpty Dumpty and candy canes would have had an instant appeal. The park sat at the entrance to the state fairgrounds from 1952 to 1987. *Rebecca Burrum collection.*

OPPOSITE: Opryland USA, no mere amusement park but a true theme park in the Disney or Six Flags style, opened in 1972. This collage from a few years later includes the tall sign that greeted arriving visitors and the logo spelled out in flowers. As mentioned many pages ago, Opryland was primarily built as the new home for the Grand Ole Opry after the long-running show left the then-sketchy neighborhood around the Ryman Auditorium. Opryland itself hung up its dulcimer after its 1997 season, but the Opry just keeps on a-goin'.

OPRYLAND
U.S.A.
. . . is Fun,
Thrills,
Rides,
Music and
a Happy Place.
HOME OF AMERICAN MUSIC
GRAND OLE OPRY

TOP: Many people have wondered why the skeleton of a Ferris wheel is visible above the trees alongside I-75 at Caryville. There seem to be as many different answers as there are askers, but the general idea is that the site was once an amusement park known as Coal Town and that there are corpses of other rides in that forest as well. Regardless, the view is a most melancholy one.

BOTTOM: Hillbilly imagery is still common in the Smokies, although perhaps not as much as in the past. This dinnerware shop on US 441 used some well-rendered versions of cartoonist Fred Lasswell's *Barney Google and Snuffy Smith* comic strip characters to decorate its signs and its exterior walls, too.

For some unexplainable reason, the fireworks stands that explode along the southern roadside more often than not pair their owner's name with some variation of "crazy" or "insane." Without delving too deeply into the psychology of that, let's just say we hope the unflattering caricature of Crazy Ann did not cause her to become a ballistic missile when she saw it. This was somewhere along US 441, but with no specific location documented. *John Margolies collection.*

WELCOME
TO
McKENZIE
HOME OF BETHEL COLLEGE
CHAMBER OF COMMERCE
PROGRESSIVE • FRIENDLY • INDUSTRIOUS

CHATTANOOGA
ALL-AMERICA CITY
Welcomes
You
Tenn. V.

OPPOSITE: Here are two examples of signs that aren't as common anymore. Both would have served as a cheery greeting to their respective areas; the one at McKenzie, in particular, has that Space Age vibe so popular at the time. At its far left, note the small sign denoting the entrance to the Brown Shoe Company plant—the manufacturer of those well-remembered Buster Brown Shoes.

ABOVE: This view of the Pigeon Forge strip in the early 1960s would be totally unrecognizable if not for the shapes of the hills in the background, which have remained unchanged by the hand of man, amazingly enough. Look closely at the signs at the left-hand side, and you'll spot the entrance to the Rebel Railroad (alias Goldrush Junction, alias Silver Dollar City, alias Dollywood), a Rock City barn and a billboard advertising the aforementioned McAfee's Court. *Mitzi Soward collection.*

In contrast to the previous shot, we might as well end with this stunning nighttime view of the same strip in the late 1980s. Note that even with all the modernization, things were still in the process of evolving, with a Cracker Barrel sign crowding next to one of the pointed-roofed KFCs, Colonel Sanders weathervane intact, and its sign with the revolving chicken bucket. And so, as the sun sets slowly in the West, we bid a fond farewell to the amazing world of vintage Tennessee signs.

BIBLIOGRAPHY

Bennett, Julie. "What Really Happened to Minnie Pearl Fried Chicken?" *Franchise Times*, June 2007.

Capps, Anita Armstrong. *See Rock City Barns: A Tennessee Tradition*. N.p.: self-published, 1996.

Escott, Colin. *The Grand Ole Opry: The Making of an American Icon*. New York: Center Street, 2006.

Hollis, Tim. *Dixie Before Disney: 100 Years of Roadside Fun*. Jackson: University Press of Mississippi, 1999.

———. *Images of Modern America: Rock City*. Charleston, SC: Arcadia Publishing, 2017.

———. *The Land of the Smokies: Great Mountain Memories*. Jackson: University Press of Mississippi, 2007.

———. *Lost Attractions of the Smoky Mountains*. Charleston, SC: The History Press, 2020.

———. *The Minibook of Minigolf*. Gainesville, FL: Seaside Publishing, 2015.

———. *See Rock City: The History of Rock City Gardens*. Charleston, SC: The History Press, 2009.

Hollis, Tim, and Mitzi Soward. *Lost Attractions of Sevier County*. Charleston, SC: Arcadia Publishing, 2011.

Jakle, John A., and Keith A. Sculle. *The Gas Station in America*. Baltimore, MD: Johns Hopkins University Press, 1994.

Jakle, John A., Keith A. Sculle and Jefferson S. Rogers. *The Motel in America*. Baltimore, MD: Johns Hopkins University Press, 1996.

Margolies, John. *Miniature Golf*. New York: Abbeville Press, 1987.

BIBLIOGRAPHY

Pearl, Minnie, with Joan Dew. *Minnie Pearl: An Autobiography*. New York: Simon and Schuster, 1980.

Sammarco, Anthony Mitchell. *A History of Howard Johnson's*. Charleston, SC: The History Press, 2013.

Thomas, Bernice L. *America's 5 & 10 Cent Stores: The Kress Legacy*. New York: John Wiley and Sons, 1997.

Wilson, Kemmons, with Robert Kerr. *Half Luck and Half Brains: The Kemmons Wilson Holiday Inn Story*. Nashville, TN: Hambleton-Hill Publishing, 1996.

ABOUT THE AUTHOR

Tim Hollis has written thirty-six books on pop-culture history, a number of them concerning southeastern tourism. He also operates his own museum of vintage toys, souvenirs and other pop-culture artifacts near Birmingham, Alabama.